The

Spiritual Notebook

By

PAUL TWITCHELL

The Spiritual Notebook

For a free book catalog write:

PUBLISHING
P.O. Box 2449
Menlo Park, CA 94025 U.S.A.

TABLE OF CONTENTS

INTRODUCTION

The Spiritual Notebook is the greatest landmark in the esoteric history of mankind, and all worlds within this universe.

It is unique in its revelation of the history of man's spiritual progress and honest in its forthright discussions of the ancient new-age doctrine of ECKANKAR which is reappearing again in this world as the truth of spiritual life.

The book takes up the study of the spiritual line of ECK Masters since the beginning of this world. For the first time we learn of these spiritually developed Masters who are adepts in the ancient order of the Vairagi. These spiritual Masters have kept themselves well hidden behind the veil of the human eyes and ears in order to get their work successfully done for mankind. It is their duty to work for individual Souls who take up the path of ECKANKAR, to be returned to the heavenly realm where they originated.

ECKANKAR is the ancient gospel which does not teach there is original sin as most orthodox religions claim. Paul Twitchell has set out to show that every prominent person in history who has contributed some beneficial good to civilization has been a chela of the hidden teachings of ECK.

He speaks with authority on the supreme message of ECK which is revealed only to those who have a simple heart. He gives the ultimate way of receiving that which is known as the God consciousness, and has the true mark of a spiritual Master. From all indications it seems that many who look for a spiritual Master do not know the true marks of those who wear this high mantle and serve the races of all people.

CHAPTER ONE

ECKANKAR, THE ANCIENT GOSPEL

Death and resurrection are the basic principles taught in almost every religion since the dawn of time. But ECKANKAR, which is the mainstream for all religions, philosophies and doctrines, was the first to show the people of the Earth, through appointed saviours, that the mystery of salvation is based on the death of the physical and the redemption of Soul.

Philosophical writers and religionists have proven the existence of ECKANKAR throughout history. The first saviour was Ramaj, who started teaching Its principles orally in the dawn of history. The famous line of prophets in the Israelite tribes were trained in the work of ECKANKAR, as their prophecies well show. The Greek masters Apollonius, Dionysius, Pythagoras, Socrates, Aristotle and Plato were taught the art of ECKANKAR by the ancient adepts. Practically every man who has contributed to civilization has been a chela, or student, of the hidden teachings of ECKANKAR. This is true of the sciences, literature, art, economy, religions, philosophies, the military, medicine, and psychology.

But in order to build a bridge between the spiritual worlds and our physical domain it is necessary to reconstruct the living chain that links our many and varied religions together. Hellenism, Christianity, and the religions of Egypt and the Middle East must have their original unity restored to them. The traditions of East and West must once again be reconciled.

The story of the saviours has been the common property of the Oriental world for thousands of years. Generally, the story is the same the lowly birth, struggles with the stormy months; the feast in the spring culminating in the crucifixion at the spring equinox, and ascendance into the spiritual heavens.

The lignt flows from one mighty founder of religion to another, from the Himalayas to the plateau of Iran, from Sinai to Tabor, from the tombs of Egypt to the sanctuary of Eleusis. The spiritual teachings held by the people of these areas have all come out of the heart of the omniscient Deity, the single Source we once knew as ECKANKAR, the ancient science of total awareness.

The great prophets, those powerful figures whom we call Rama, Krishna, Hermes, Moses, Orpheus, Pythagoras, Plato and Jesus, are known to have been chelas in the various mystery schools—such as the Essene—which are all offsprings of the ancient order of ECKANKAR Masters, known most commonly as the Order of the Vairagi Avatars.

They are diverse in form, appearance and color. Nevertheless, through all of them moves the impulse of the eternal ECK, or the eternal Word. To be in harmony with them is to hear and see the Word—God—in action.

The Supreme Message can be revealed ultimately to those simple in heart. Its starting point lies where Truth pushes aside the cloak of illusion, and becomes the shining inspiration to initiates of ECKANKAR. The link-up of the individual Soul with the essence of the spiritual Word gives the initiate an insight into the great mysteries of heaven and earth.

The need for spiritual works is universally human, and any individual who assumes he can live without an accompanying spiritual advancement is caught in a self-deceptive trap. Only through the spiritual travelers in the worlds beyond can one find success in the works of the SUGMAD.

The four races that share the globe today are the daughters and sons of varied lands. By successive creations, slow elaborations of the earth at work, the continents have emerged from the seas at great intervals of time. These intervals the ancient priests of India called the interdiluvian cycles. During thousands of years each continent produced its flora and fauna, culminating in a human race of different color.

The Southern continent, engulfed by the last great flood, was the cradle of the primitive red race, of which the Ameri-

6

can Indians are descendents. They are the remnants of the Troglodytes, who reached the top of gigantic mountains when their continent sank.

Africa is the home of the black race, called the Ethiopians by the Greeks. Asia gave birth to the yellow race, as preserved in the Chinese. The white race came last, from the forests of Europe, between the tempests of the Atlantic and the mild world of the Mediterranean. All human types are the results of mixtures, combinations, degeneracies or selections of these four great races.

In preceding cycles the red and the black races ruled successively with powerful civilizations. They left reminders of their supremacy in gigantic ruins, such as the templed structures of Mexico. At the present time the white race has ruled for a long cycle, and if one looks at the antiquity of India and Egypt, one will find that its preponderance dates back seven or eight thousand years.

According to the Hindu traditions, civilization began on the Southern continent while all of Europe and part of Asia were under water. The red race inhabited that part of the Southern continent we know as Atlantis. Atlantis was eventually destroyed by a great earthquake, scattering its people. The Polynesians, North American Indians and the Aztecs are descendents of the race that once inhabited this now sunken continent.

Following the breakup of the red race, the black race took dominance over the known world. They came out of the region known today as Ethiopia, and established their supremacy on the Mediterranean shores. This black movement precipitated a migration of the Aryan [white race] out of Central Asia and into Iran, India, and countries of the Far East, to establish the first Aryan civilization. They mixed with the red, black, and yellow races.

During this period men gained ascendancy over women in religious knowledge. The ancient scriptures tell us that no one had the right to speak except the rishis and prophets. Women became subjugated, and were no longer a part of the religious group even as priestesses, as they had been in Egypt.

7

Yet here, too, the black race made their women slaves, and the priests semi-gods.

In Europe, however, among the white races, the woman was still an important part of religious life. She was a prophetess at the many oracles, as evidenced by the pythoness, who gave to the Greeks predictions that governed their nation. There were also Druidesses who went into battle with their German armies, and many others who were accepted as rulers of the inner life for their nations and tribes.

The yellow race had its years of supremacy in Asia, but it concentrated its attention within its own borders, and those of Southeast Asia and Japan.

The white races then overthrew the black cities that had been established on the European coasts, and later invaded North Africa and Central Asia. They released the slaves of the black men, who had been forced into helping create an advanced civilization. Part of this advancement was due to the art of holy writing, which was the recording of spiritual ideas by means of certain strange hieroglyphic signs on animal skins, stone, or tree bark.

It was at this point that ECKANKAR split off from more general teachings. Instead of becoming a written dogma it continued to be transmitted through oral instruction alone. The ECK Masters occasionally relayed messages to groups of chelas, but more often they chose to hand down the knowledge of ECK through secret teachings to an individual student.

The knowledge of how to melt iron ore to make weapons, and the use of writing, were taken over by the white race, who had conquered the black cities in Europe. The mixing of these two races produced the Semitic race, whose peoples include the Menes, Egyptians, Arabs, Phoenicians, Chaldeans and Jews.

Thus the Middle East became the belt of a mixed race, which in turn became a great river of philosophical, scientific and religious thought. Out of this region came the sacred scriptures of the Jewish Torah, the Islamic Koran, Mithraism, and many others of Semitic origin. At the same time

8

Aryan thought produced the Zend-Avesta, Ramayana, that is, the Hindu sacred writings; the Vedas, and Buddhism.

All of these sacred writings, which were the ancestors of modern religions and philosophies, sprang from the oral fountainhead known as ECKANKAR. ECKANKAR is the All-Embracing Force, the spiritual Source of everything that comprises life. This is why we follow the path of ECKANKAR, for it is the mainstream and closest to the pure teachings derived from the Ocean of Love and Mercy, or God, poetically speaking.

The Semitic and Aryan races can be viewed as two great rivers that have flowed down through the ages. Upon both have floated great ideas of mythology, religion, art, science and philosophy.

But the Semitic and Aryan currents have carried two different conceptions of life. The reconciliation and balance of the two is said to be truth, but this is not necessarily so. ECKANKAR is the only current of life, and it alone carries the full conception of truth.

The Semitic current provides absolutes and superior principles which is the idea of unity and universality in the name of a supreme Principle(called Allah, God, and other names) in its application to the unification of the human family. The Aryan current provides the concept of ascending evolution in all terrestial and supra-terrestial kingdoms into the richness of advancing development.

The basis of Semitic thinking is that spirit descends from God into man, thus becoming the God-man on Earth. The Aryan principle is that spirit within man ascends from man to God, thus unfolding spiritually until Soul becomes one with God. The first is represented by the avenging archangel who descends from heaven with his sword and thunder; the other by the spiritually developed Soul who is able to take the elements from heaven to help the human race in its struggle to have life more abundantly.

Man bears these two principles within himself. He thinks and acts under the influence of one or the other in turn, for they are not harmoniously blended within him. They contradict and fight one another on the battleground of our inner feelings, in our subtle thoughts, as well as in our social life and institutions. Hidden beneath our many social forms and mores are the currents which we may call spirituality and naturalism. They control our arguments and struggles.

We can look through all the past fronts of history to the age of Moses in Egypt, where thirty thousand years ago the Semitic principles seem to have been born. At about the same time the Aryan race entered India and established its own principles, becoming also the first known civilization. Both are said to be founders of religions. Yet both were well acquainted with the great initiation, which is the foundation for entering into the spiritual worlds.

We can trace the works of both down through the ages, seeing how the Aryan influence in the tradition of the Vedas became a higher civilization spreading out of India, eastward into Persia, Greece, and finally into the northern countries of Europe. We can also note the route taken by the Semitic teachings which came through Moses into the Middle Eastern world. These original teachings of Judaism came finally to Jesus who, like Buddha in the East, then reformed the religious and traditional Semitic beliefs into a modern concept for every man. Finally the outer form, which has become Christianity for the Western mind, has practically covered the globe.

Many religious scholars, including the adepts, say that the two streams are irreconcilable, invincible, and will not be united. But they fail to look beyond the outer forms of these two streams. Like most scholars—and even mystics who follow but one path—they seem to have a dualistic, and perhaps a fatalistic, attitude towards these two opposing streams of life. This has been proved by the conflict between the Occidental and Oriental worlds, from ancient Sumaria to modern Russia.

These conflicting streams of thought appear so much in our lives that usually we fail to recognize them. Hence, newspapers, books and discussions are filled with the seesaw between the two worlds. And, as stated previously, the individual must fight his own inner battles over these opposing streams of life. History has proved that the bloody conflicts between most nations can be boiled down to the opposing ideas of Semitic and Aryan concepts.

I have stated that ECKANKAR is the All-Embracing Force of life, and our whole elemental living is made up from within the worlds of God. Those seeking the ultimate experience, or God-Realization, have no judgment of which path to take. This is because most individuals do not have a criterion by which to judge their inner experiences. We live too much in the external, always taking the objective, outer viewpoint, to know much about the inner life and its effects upon our spiritual behaviour.

Most of us are not very good at understanding ourselves. We are like the young woman who told Michaelangelo Antonioni, the Italian cinematic director-producer, (whose films are based upon the spiritually bankrupted world), that she would like to smoke pot in the Cathedral of St. Mark in Venice, Italy, because it would greatly augment her pleasure of its beauty.

There was nothing profane about her desire to smoke marijuana in a sacred spot. She merely wanted to make her aesthetic emotions more intense. But because she was ignorant of the natural ways to do it she chose marijuana, a drug, which is only an artificial means. Drugs are but another mask hiding the true underlying way to God, the path of ECKANKAR.

ECKANKAR is hidden in all things, but we hardly see It cloaked behind the Semitic and Aryan streams of life. In a way we are like Alice in Wonderland who, upon leaving the Duchess' abode, did not know what direction to take. She asked the Cheshire Cat which way she should walk and he told her that it depended on where she wanted to go. Alice said that it did not matter as long as she got somewhere, to which the cat replied that she would do so if she only walked long enough.

This is how we search for the Divine Reality, God, that Ocean of Love and Mercy. We bumble around taking any path, whether it is Shintoism, Judaism, Christianity, Islamism, Hinduism, Buddhism, Taoism, Confucianism or Jainism. We fumble through the outer forms of religions and the mysteries of the Cabala, Eleusis, and many others. In the end we come to the same conclusion reached by a friend of mine, just prior to her death. After following an Indian guru for years she said,

"I have spent over thirty years being a good person, leading a good life, practicing meditation daily, listening to my Guru and following his instructions. I have fasted, been a vegetarian, been chaste, been initiated, done everything given me in the instructions, but I have not advanced spiritually one iota. I have not seen the Light of God nor heard His Voice. What could have gone wrong?"

This story is the oldest tale told by a religious follower. Either he takes one path and fails; or he bargain shops, picking over everything possible, and again ends up a failure. This happens because he fails to look behind the facade of all the many masks placed before him. He fails to see the divine ECKANKAR following him as the All-Embracing Life Current; vitalizing him, lifting him, and trying to say: "Come follow me!"

Even many who manage to find ECKANKAR fail because they judge it by their own experience. They have preconceived notions of what it must do for them, and are disappointed when these false expectations are not realized. Here, too, as in so many other circumstances, the maxim applies: "It is not what ECKANKAR will do for you, but what you can do for ECKANKAR."

This is the basic principle of ECKANKAR, that forms the foundation of life. Too many of us want life to do something for us. We call upon God to give us material and spiritual things; then, when our prayers go amiss, we are apt to turn away to something that seems to offer more in the way of miracles.

Another foundation of life is love. This word, like meditation, has unfortunately been so overworked that we are often misled by the clergy and acolytes. We are told to love and love regardless of what happens to us. Yet love is conflict, obvious and natural. There is hardly a piece of literature or sacred writing that is not based on the conquest of happiness, or the effort to arrive at what we call love. It is the struggle that appears to interest those who produce works of art, literature, cinema and poetry. But who can give any absolute definition of what love is, or even whether it ought to exist?

Love can best be classified as a dichotomy. Its opposite is hate—as beauty is the opposite of ugliness—and all other abstracts are contained therein. We are not following these abstracts, though, but the highest known Force, the All-Embracing ECKANKAR. Thus the dynamics of ECKANKAR are not included in the works of love, for ECKANKAR is the dynamic of the absolute God, or the divine vortex. When we see It working in others and observe It within ourselves, we find that all life is changed. Reality becomes something quite different from anything that we have been taught, have read about, or experienced in the lower worlds of consciousness.

When we step into this state of consciousness life becomes a whole. Nothing remains in the dichotomic pattern; all things are singular. Love as we knew it is nothing—only an offspring of religious teachings—and we live in a state of vairag, or detachment. In particular, we experience a mental detachment from love of the world, and from all worldly desires.

This should not, however, imply asceticism. It means joy in living and not being disturbed by the things of this world. It is something dynamic, and unlike the ideas of the Semitic and Aryan currents that govern this physical world.

So far, our definition of ECKANKAR reads "The All-Embracing spiritual Force of the SUGMAD which composes life and makes up all elemental substances, including the component parts of Soul. It is the audible life Force that we can hear and see with the spiritual vision and objective sight of materialism."

ECKANKAR created and comprises all the religious ideas

of the lower worlds. Art, writing, music and sculpture are only developments of the higher ideals of ECKANKAR. ECKANKAR serves as a wheel, whose spokes run out to the rim upon which the vehicle is carried.

This wheel illustrates how the major religions of the world have sprung out of ECKANKAR. Named here are twelve spokes in the Wheel of ECKANKAR. They are: Animism, Hinduism, Islam, Christianity, Judaism, Shintoism, Buddhism, Taoism, Jainism, Zoroastrianism, Mystery cults, and Sufism.

The spokes represent each world religion of importance to individuals today. They can also represent the various philosophies that have grown out of these religions, but there is little need to delineate them. There is ample evidence that none of these religions, which are supposed to give us comfort and succor, are successful with everybody. This is why the divine SUGMAD is divided into twelve spokes. Mainly due to our individual training in this world, we have to go the route to heaven in our own manner, along the path that is best suited for us, but in the end its always the path of ECK.

This is why some people have failed in ECKANKAR. They are not yet ready for it, mainly due to a lack of spiritual evolution. Many times, too, preconceived ideas about ECKANKAR and misunderstandings of the basic principles in life will obstruct an individual's progress.

These preconceived notions are established largely by metaphysical teachers who are giving us the wrong principles of life. They tell us that nothing is impossible; that once we experience God everything becomes well with us, and we can have everything we desire. Such teachings are only broad, general statements, not even worth the paper they are written upon for eyes to see and the mind to study. This is the worst kind of pampering for an individual in our modern times. It makes us the target of unscrupulous sales people who are only looking for commercial values with which to produce returns for their own comfort and convenience.

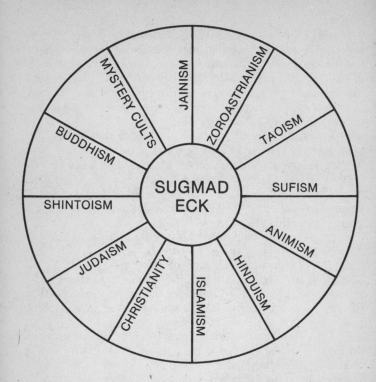

THE WHEEL OF ECKANKAR

The major religions of the world have sprung out of ECKANKAR. Named here are twelve spokes in the Wheel of ECKANKAR. They are: Animism, Hinduism, Islamism, Christianity, Judaism, Shintoism, Buddhism, Taoism, Jainism, Zoroastrianism, Mystery Cults, and Sufism.

The spokes represent each world religion of importance to the individual, today. Also, they can represent the various philosophies which have grown out of the religions. None of these religions, which are supposed to give us comfort and succor, is successful with everybody. This is why the Divine SUGMAD is divided into the twelve spokes. We have to go the route to heaven in our own manner, along the path that is best suited for us, eventually entering into ECKANKAR as the final way.

Hence, a student of ECKANKAR cannot be bothered with lower laws, except those that must be abided by in order to live within society and with our neighbors. We must look at life through the overall view of ECKANKAR, which sees and knows all things. This is the three-hundred-sixty degree viewpoint that I have spoken of so often throughout the propagation of ECKANKAR.

The central issue that must be dealt with now is that too many people look at ECKANKAR as a means only to projection. This is a semantical error made by too many people who have limited their thinking to lower plane projection, for ECKANKAR has nothing to do with projection. These people have accepted astral projection but stubbornly refuse to see beyond this plane.

If we were concerned only with this phenomenon we would do well to stop right there, for life in the astral world entails only another limited state of being. We would be as limited in life there as we are limited in the physical body here, on this plane. It is important, therefore, to realize that we are not projecting, but moving from one state of consciousness to other states of consciousness.

If from childhood we had been trained to be thieves, then this would be the state of consciousness in which we would live and abide. But if this conditioning within us as thieves were changed to include becoming a doctor or a dentist who serves the public, then we would have moved from a lower state to a higher one. This is what projection actually is: the moving from one state to another.

We are like children who read and dream of leading the romantic life of a pirate, a cowboy, or something equally dramatic, but then must return to reality when the schoolbell rings. We can think and live in the state of God-consciousness with full awareness, but until we enter into a permanent state of Being, each return to the actual events of our physical lives will be seen to be a let down.

We can project ourselves into this state of God-consciousness, but to stay there we must learn to retain our full awareness of it while continuing to carry out the daily affairs of

16

life. Only then can we consider ourselves successful in our attempt at living the life in God.

I am trying to give everyone who can read a means to self-evaluation and a method of understanding his inner experiences. It is absurd to put all our energies into the reality of books, study, and discussion, for only through our own inner experiences can these things be truly known. No matter how many books we read or how many teachers we talk to, we cannot truly evaluate either unless we know how to judge our own inward experiences. And, we cannot judge the insights of the printed page or a teacher's conversation without having first had insight into ourselves.

The struggle for life is not only a religious and philosophical one, but one of divine knowledge, too. This knowledge provides us with a permanency of understanding and remains an eternal source of happiness.

All these things can be learned through the medium of ECKANKAR, the only and universal path to God.

When we come to the final analysis of life, we realize that ECKANKAR will provide us with the whole spectrum. It, of Itself, is the All-Embracing and universal path to God. All others are contained within Its fold, and we are the Children of Light and the victims of semantics.

CHAPTER Two

CONSCIOUSNESS IS THE ONLY STATE
WORTH CONSIDERATION

A Master earns the authority to wear his spiritual mantle and to speak with divine confidence and wisdom by establishing himself in the state of God consciousness. This is the mark of the true spiritual Master, of whom I have spoken so often in ECK lectures and seminars. The true spiritual Master is the Sat-Guru, the Light-bearer for this physical universe. He is sometimes called the Param Sant [meaning the Supreme One] because he has reached the highest possible attainment in supreme God consciousness.

In order to give out truth and knowledge to the chelas traveling the path of ECK, it is necessary to take up the designation of those highly developed ones serving in the spiritual hierarchy of the ancient Order of the Vairagis. These are the ECK Masters.

The true ECK Master is a Sat-Guru appointed by the Supreme Deity we know as Sat Nam, ruler of the Soul, or fifth plane, and all worlds above and below it. He is the first manifestation of God, the ultimate SUGMAD. Therefore, it is Sat Nam who appoints each Sat-Guru on the various planes throughout the spiritual heirarchy. But the Sat-Guru in the material universe today, whom we can see and talk with in the physical form, is our chief spiritual authority. He speaks for God on every plane through all the universes, from the lowest negative to the highest spiritual one.

His place here is to contact and uplift all humanity. He is responsible only to God, often bypassing Sat Nam, the Vi-Guru. I have given several lectures on this phase of the true spiritual Master under the title, "The Two Faces of the Master," referring to the inner Master and the outer Master.

The Sat-Guru is the Son of God. This same expression was used to describe Christ during His stay on Earth. It meant that he was directly responsible to the Supreme Deity, and it was only he who could bypass all planes to lead the chela into the heavenly worlds again. It also means that there is never a time in all the world ages that we do not have a Sat-Guru with us.

It is difficult to understand a Sat-Guru, but those following the supreme path of ECK know the true spiritual Master. They know who is leading the world today, who is uplifting and giving spiritual enlightenment in this age. The true marks of the world teacher are given in the first part of the first discourse, "The Precepts of ECKANKAR." A study of these marks will enlighten any chela and help him recognize the true Master.

Briefly, we will now take up a study of the different degrees of highly developed persons whom we call spiritual masters. First, we will speak of the Mahatma which is a title often given to the Sat-Guru. In India, it should be pointed out, it is a word often used very loosely, and generally meaning anyone who has attained some degree of religious eminence.

The Mahatma is a word taken from two parts, a prefix meaning maha, great, and a suffix meaning atma, Soul. Thus the word means "great Soul." A yogi is a Mahatma of a much lower degree than a Sat-Guru, and of course, a guru is generally of a much lower scale. A yogi practices a certain system of exercises through which he hopes to attain union with God. This practice is called yoga. Union with God is not, however, what we as followers of the path of ECK are seeking.

Union with God is but a phrase meaning that the practitioner expects to be swallowed up by the Supreme Deity and become a passive atom, without any self-determination or freedom of choice. On the other hand, the follower of ECK expects to become a co-worker with God. He expects to become active in spiritual tasks, with determination and freedom of choice duly awarded him. This same concept forms

20

the basis of the Hindu religious experience. Accordingly, we must decide whether we want to be influenced by some sort of materiality or go into the heavenly worlds.

The majority of yogis, including ancient and contemporary, have only reached the first step on the path of ECK. They have scarcely achieved the astral plane, yet they do not know this. This means that we must consider the argument that a spiritual system which has gained popularity among the masses may be one of the worst paths to take. Any system that is popular is hardly a true path to heaven.

The Mahatmas can be divided into several classes. First is the Acolyte, or one who has reached the first step on the path to the SUGMAD. He is able to dwell in the astral plane among the inhabitants of its city, Sahasra-dal-Kanwal.

Second is the Sadhu, or one who has attained the third region. Often, in India, he is considered the thrice born and wears a triple thread on his arm. This is done to show that he has dedicated himself to the quest for spiritual enlightenment, and has renounced all worldly goods and comfort.

Third is the Sant, or the Adept. The Adept is one who has not only attained the Soul plane, but has established himself there. He becomes a Master of spiritual knowledge, an agent of God, and is able to move anywhere in the spiritual universes as he desires. He is the inner and outer Master of whom I have spoken so much. The Christians, in their Bible, give the title of Christ to the Adept, while the Buddhists call him the Buddhi. Many other recognized titles in various religions are fastened to the Adept.

Fourth is the ECKshar, or the supreme Sant. He has reached the highest attainment in the God region. These degrees of unfoldment into God, let it be pointed out, are not conferred degrees, but are recognized stages of spiritual experiences. They are gained by Soul's ability to stay with the path of ECK, and by paramount faith in the lofty ideals of ECKANKAR.

Many religious orders have fixed degrees of spiritual unfoldment into perfection. The Buddhists, for example, con-

21

fer the title of Bodhisattva unto those who have gone through the ten stages of unfoldment on the path to Buddhism, or perfection. But the fact that spiritual perfection does not stop with ten stages or even a thousand stages makes this a pseudo-claim. There is always a plus element in the attainment of spiritual perfection. There is always another step to take, regardless of the achievement we have made already. If one should attain complete spiritual perfection then he would replace God, and this would be not only impossible and impractical, but highly preposterous.

There are many other titles on a lower spiritual scale. These have been adopted and attached to travelers who have had some attainment in the spirito-materialistic worlds, that is, physical, astral, causal and mental. A Rishi is one whose development follows a growth pattern similar to that of a yogi. A Maha Rishi is superior to those who have gained the singular title of Rishi, but he is not a spiritual Master. The Sat-Guru, the Sant, Sadhu and the ECKshar are so far superior to the Rishi and the Maha Rishi that there is no comparison. The Vi Guru is the higher title, and the Mahanta, the Living Master, the highest.

Many other titles are given by different religious orders. The Mursheed, for example, is supposedly a Master among the Muslims and Sufis. These titles are often applied, however, to men who are neither saints nor Masters.

As pointed out earlier in this chapter, a Sant, or Master, is one who has reached the fifth region. This is the Soul plane, sometimes called the Sach Khand. A Sant has reached Soul perfection for Self-Realization within the Order of the Vairagi Masters.

The Mahanta is the highest one can go in these lower worlds. He is a god man, appointed by the divine SUGMAD for the purpose of giving the Nam, the Word, of the initiation. His chief duty is to show those who enter into initiation the road back to heaven again. He also serves as a guide.

The Sat-Guru is the authority for the SUGMAD. He is what the Christians know in their Gospel as the Son of God.

In other words, he is the trinity discussed in the New Testament and other religious writings of the world. He is the one who has reached the stage of the God State.

That authority should be placed upon the one who becomes the saviour is not unusual. In Egypt the Pharoah of old was both a god and the son of a god, and Krishna, the beloved god of India, was one of countless sun gods. Many men have become gods and many gods have become men. But the Mahanta is the living Light, in the tradition of the ancient sun gods of Asia.

He may walk the Earth unknown, but still he is the saviour god, after the manner of Osiris, Attis and Mithra. Like them he belongs by origin to the celestial world; like them he makes his appearance on Earth and accomplishes a work of universal redemption. Like the ancient gods Adonis, Osiris, Attis and Krishna, he often dies of strange death and then is restored to life.

As in the tradition of all these sun gods his advent and the events of his life are predestined. His way is prepared, and the salvation of those who share his suffering and passion for life and freedom, is assured.

We are the individual embodiment of the trinity, spoken of so much by the Christians. By this I mean that each person is spirit, mind and body—the three in one and one in three. So it is with God, spirit, mind and body. Three in one and one in three.

Within spirit we find happiness, awareness and action; in mind there is thought, volition and seeking; and in body there is the sensual search for happiness. If we dwell in spirit, or Soul, we are living in happiness, for Soul is a happy entity. It is seldom anything else. When the mind presses in on it too strongly, however, it withdraws and leaves the body under the tyranny of mind.

To enter into the heavenly kingdom, then, we must do it consciously, and in order to do this we must practice our spiritual exercises consciously. We do not bring down the kingdom of heaven but lift ourselves into those spiritual planes. This is all done consciously, by our own volition. In this way we also develop grace, and through this attribute of God comes love for all things.

It is states of consciousness that we are working with, nothing else. These states are: (1) spirit, (2) subconscious, (3) mind, and (4) body. Man is the distributor of the divine ECK, but It reaches into the objective world only in accordance with his state of consciousness. This means that if man is working with true spiritual power he will become a channel for It. He can also be a channel for negative power, but this depends entirely upon the state in which he habitually rests.

When we begin to enter into spiritual consciousness and by habit live there, we are no longer seeking. It is possible to enter this state with the aid of others. A man can ride into the other worlds on his friends' thought streams, making him a highly spiritual man. But if one within this group begins to doubt or be filled with suspicion, our man can also be pushed down to the bottom of the ladder.

The art of questioning is hardly more than theorizing. Therefore, those who simply run from one teacher to another are still dealing in theory, and not in practice. Those who ask questions, who read books and other forms of literature, are following out theory. Not until one begins to practice and apply does he start to succeed in the works of ECK.

Theory is only the initial step towards reaching the God State. Yet all together there are three important aspects in ECK. First, we must study the books, literature and discourses in order to learn the theory of ECKANKAR. Second, we must put into practice the spiritual exercises laid down in the discourses. This practice must be continued over a long period of time, perhaps over years. It must be done, though, for we cannot learn to discipline ourselves without practice. Third, we must pass through the books and discourses to become initiates. On this level we find that the secret knowledge begins to enter into the consciousness of the initiate without as great an effort as was formerly required. He no longer seeks but just IS!

24

A strange phenomenon exists, however, during the first two stages of the neophyte. He must pay for everything he receives, either in the form of money or some other kind of exchange. This is something that must be done, for the seeker is on the lower levels and cannot thrust himself into the highest realms until he has unfolded properly. Once the seeker has passed these first two stages and has entered into the third aspect he no longer leans upon books, discourses, and other writings. But he does have to serve as a channel for the divine ECK to pour down through him into the outer worlds. In this way he is never charged for any knowledge received, be it from books or via a higher state of consciousness. He has now become the ECK, of Itself.

Everyone understands ECKANKAR according to the level of his own consciousness. This consciousness is established early in life, between the ages of one and six. It is shaped mainly by his mother's teachings, his training, his heredity, environment, genealogy, and his early educational instructions. The rest of his experiences in life are mostly materialistic pedagogics.

Unless an individual is brought into the teachings of ECK, most of the work given him will be scarcely worth anything. Left to himself, the character traits man develops for his adult life are apt to be mostly negative and destructive to himself. These traits are held in check only by the social order in which one lives.

It is for the above reasons that everybody who listens to or reads about ECK interprets according to his own level of consciousness. A Christian will see in it the light of his training, and a Moslem will look at it through the screen of his particular religious understanding. This all too human habit has caused many ECK Masters to keep the truth of ECK an invisible side of their teachings. The people of their times did not have the right level of consciousness to accept the full truth.

Water has to seek its own level, according to science. ECK is in somewhat the same position, for it must seek to express Itself through a state of consciousness which is ready to receive It. The degree of expression will depend upon the level of consciousness.

To some people ECK will appear as spiritualism, to others as some form of cultism, and to still others as a highly complex religious body like the Buddhist or Catholic faiths. ECK takes advantage of whatever opening is available to It, be it a single or collective state of consciousness. Outwardly, ECK makes Its appearance wrapped in the rituals, elegant trapping and utterances of the founders. A closer examination will show, however, that ECK is hidden in the written scriptures and sacred literature of the world's religious bodies.

The ECK seeps into every state of consciousness, regardless of its level. In every manner of experience it will somehow appear, whether it is in diluted form or the full truth. To receive the full truth, however, we must experience the supreme state of consciousness.

Never is the experience of God decided together. Such depths of knowing come only to the alone with the Alone. This is why those who are known as saviours, savants, men of God, or gurus often look so lonely, especially the eyes. They have seen and felt the suffering of the world races, but they are alone. No one can give one of these love or life save the Supreme Deity. Too often the SUGMAD will leave such a one alone to work out his own dark nights of the Soul.

This is why ECKANKAR is an individual path. All may travel it, but not as a collective group. Each must go his own way and experience that which is his own. This is also why ECK is usually for the advanced chela, for unless he has gained enough understanding of the ways of ECK he will always be dependent on the Master.

The Master knows that no one in the physical body can escape death, although many are trying to do so. We cannot find anyone on which it never lights, nor anyone who has a charm against it. Only a few, only the handful who have learned the secret of ECK, have found that they can escape death; all others must learn to escape the fear of it.

26

Therefore, all we are here concerned with is states of consciousness. When Paul, the great ECK Master, was writing his famous letters recorded in the New Testament, he said in the "Epistle to the Ephesians," "All things that are reproved are made manifest by the Light; for whatsoever doth make manifest is Light."

What he is telling us here is that Light is consciousness. Consciousness is one, or what the Hindus speak of as unity, but it manifests in millions of forms and levels of consciousness. This is what I was speaking of earlier when I said that the ECK seeks its own level with whatever state the individual is dwelling in, and accepts that state as part of the divine spirit, or ECK.

There is no separation of consciousness for the ECK cannot be divided into parts. We are all there is in consciousness, yet few or none have realized that they exist as a whole, or one. This is the state of self-recognition, which I have often pointed out as knowing what IS. In truth, we find that there is no reality outside ourselves.

The state in which one dwells may be good, bad, or indifferent, but it has nothing to do with the wholeness of ECK. We will become that which we conceive ourselves to be. Or, in other words, the consciousness within us will take on the manifestation of whatever we desire ourselves to be, either in form or manifested thought. Consciousness is a law unto itself, which manifests at our command. We are the law and shape our states of consciousness as we desire.

Once we establish our states of being in the higher self, then we are free from the tyranny of second causes, and free from the belief that causes outside ourselves can affect us.

Consciousness is spirit, and the ECK that dwells within us is also consciousness, or spirit. The best example of this is the novel. A novel is only a state of consciousness, as is any non-fiction book. Travel to another place is also a state of consciousness, for if home is different from New York, we would expect to find a different state of consciousness there. This is true of any city in the world, and of any foreign country, for customs and traditions lend variety to the different states of collective thought in each one. Now, if man has established different levels of consciousness throughout the world, in cities, states and countries, we have a strong case for declaring that the other spiritual planes are merely states of consciousness, too.

This world can be viewed as being an infinite number of states of consciousness. Accordingly, those worlds beyond the physical can be seen as a continuation of those countless levels of consciousness. The lowest states are in the physical world, but they grow brighter and exceedingly more exquisite as we travel through them to the God State. We are not actually traveling, in the normal sense of the word, but we are experiencing what is known as being there. We know this. Nothing can change our faith and happiness in this knowledge. It is again a recognition of the state we are dwelling in, and the realization that we shall never separate ourselves from this state.

The worlds beyond are states of consciousness that we move into as Souls, not bodies. We never travel in either the astral, causal or mental bodies, but always as Soul, the real self. This is the reality of life and must be accepted as such. In Soul Travel, what we are really working with are the fields of awareness and recognition. When we enter into the next plane we become aware of it, recognize whatever is there for us to view, and retain complete perceptions of that world.

We are free to choose our own states of consciousness as dwelling planes, but we usually end up crying to be saved from the state of our choice. All of these states are lifeless until we enter into them and become one with each. This is the whole secret of life: to enter into a state of consciousness and become one with it. Therefore, when we enter into the astral world we are to become one with it, or achieve unity with it as a state of being. If we instead project there in the astral body, the silver cord will be part of the equipment we will have to take along. If we move into this state via the original method of Soul Travel, however, we are free of any excess baggage, such as the silver cord. We are traveling as free agents.

Let me point out once more, though, that we are not traveling in the usual sense of the word, but experiencing self-recognition, and living in the sense of the desire fulfilled. Therefore, if we desire to dwell on any of the other planes — or even in the state of God-consciousness — we must live with the attitude of the wish fulfilled. This is the knowingness that makes all things come true.

Travel such as this is known as inner movement. Our inner self is as real in the subjective world as the physical body is in the world of external things. But the inner self expresses a far more fundamental part of consciousness. This inner self is like the outer one, though, for it must be consciously directed and disciplined through the spiritual exercises of ECK.

The subjective world of thought and feeling is attuned to the spiritual self of man. It has its own structure and contains living entities in its own higher places. The movement of the spiritual self, Soul, is always causal. What moves it is the inner action that we desire to apply for the subjective experience. All this subjective movement is caused by the action taking place independently of outer body action.

In this way movement is made possible on any plane, because the outer body can never follow. It is only the independent action of the subjective self that is in motion and has freedom. This is what makes the Master different from one who has not yet reached this state of perfection. The Master has control over his inner body and can move it anywhere without obstacles and barriers standing in the way.

The person who is not trained will allow himself to be carried away by negativity, which will bring him under the control of the Kal forces. He is likely to be filled with negative, mechanical chattering, and is disturbed over many things arising on the outer external side. He cannot obtain the proper subjective experiences because he cannot control himself inwardly. This is why I have repeatedly stressed that discipline brings freedom. Once we find the key to controlling the motion of the inner self, then freedom becomes our state of consciousness. We have freedom of choice: to

29

make any decision, travel in any world, and become one who dwells in the God State constantly.

This is why I keep emphasizing the importance of the spiritual exercises of ECK. For even though many people go through the courses offered them, there are still those who feel that, because nothing comes with a few trial efforts, either they themselves are not ready for Soul Travel, or the exercises are not the least bit worthy of practice.

It is not at all unusual for someone to write me expressing dissatisfaction because they practiced the first drill for two days and nothing came of it. This is the lazy man's way of doing things. We do not expect to attend school for a mere two days and learn the whole of geometry. Relatively few learn the discipline of ECK within so short a period of time.

The struggle between the two orders of the world keeps going on, and we are quite overcome by what we term the outer, or negative self, which takes control of our actions. Therefore, in order to be in possession of ourselves and have our freedom, it is imperative that we take on the difficult task of self-discipline. Unless we do so there will never be any freedom, and we shall lack the opportunity of inner movement into the higher states of consciousness.

When we come to the realization that spirit is the underlying cause to all effects, other bits of learning fall into place. Among these is the knowledge that we can have no dependency on either persons or things, but only on the ECK. It is this inner power that will shape our whole lives and become manifested through our states of consciousness into the outer world.

To reach this state we do not use denials, affirmations, prayer, rituals, nor any of the many other forms of outer discipline. None of these can help us, for we must strive to reach perfection through the spiritual exercises of ECK. Tradition, habit, customs, environment and heredity will imprison anyone, leaving him unable to do the work in disciplining the inner self.

Let me stress that this is not a mental discipline. It is a discipline of the emotional feelings and imaginative forces.

If one faithfully follows the spiritual exercises he will see them taking over in this continued contest between will power and the imaginative forces. In the end we find that the imagination will win, always, for it is the generator of emotion.

This is what self-discipline entails; the control of the subjective self. But it will not take place until the control we place over it is strict, for imagination can also bring fear, unhappiness, and all the negative qualities of life. We must always remember, though, that under control it can give us love, freedom and happiness.

Therefore, if I should say that "My kingdom is not of this world," I would mean that I live in that state of consciousness where everything is beauty, Light and Sound. Anyone who reaches this state realizes that he will be under constant attack from the negative force, which would like to pull him back down. This is why those living in the higher states are able to give love in return for the assaults on themselves from loved ones and strangers. They know that they must in order to retain that plane of existence.

Consciousness is therefore the only state we know worth consideration in our study of ECK.

CHAPTER THREE

THE WAYS TRUTH REACHES ALL
PEOPLE AND THINGS

Truth has its own peculiar way of reaching the objective world through the individual consciousness of every living thing. This includes the consciousness of minerals, stones, plants, and animals, as well as man.

The supreme SUGMAD pervades the macrocosm by the Name and Word, or what we call "The SUGMAD and ECK." God, or the SUGMAD, is present also in the microcosm. Its Name and ECK, though all-pervading, cannot be experienced by the physical senses of any living thing. It must be experienced via the consciousness.

If this is so, then we must realize that the real spiritual form is distorted by the senses. The mind experiences the objective world through the physical senses. Therefore, the inner universe cannot be realized unless we are able to separate Soul from mind and physical senses, and visualize Truth directly. This is possible if one follows the path of ECK.

ECK can be the universal path of man, but he makes it difficult. This difficulty is caused largely by a lack of knowledge that it existed and lack of will to follow it. These two difficulties, however, are easily solved by the appearance of the Mahanta, the living ECK Master, or one who has followed the true path and realized Truth.

No man has solved the problems of life by philosophy, religion or mysticism. Regardless of what so many in these three fields of spiritual endeavor have said or written, none have been able to give Truth. The totality of spiritual experience lies in the heart of the ECK. It is only when one has entered into the ECK and become the instrument of God that he knows about Truth.

Truth uses man for Its divine purpose by entering into

his lower consciousness and enlightening him. This is done for the purpose of evolving man spiritually so that he can continue to unfold. Truth lifts man through the veils of daily death.

Each time we pass the veil of death into another plane beyond the physical, we die in the lower state of consciousness. A new concept of life is born, and we are given a deeper and broader view of all things beyond the human senses. And, when we have reached the end of the road in this life, we must pass on into the great beyond with no fear of death. Through the preparatory experience of daily death we act with a natural tendency to accept other planes as part of our eternal journey.

Occasionally I receive letters from persons who are just embarking upon what we call old age. They are fearful of death because to them it represents nothing but a dark world, one in which there is nothing but black nothingness. They understand death only as stepping across the line of physical life into something unknown, much as the ancient people believed that beyond the Rock of Gibraltar was only a world of nothingness.

I have always tried to get it across to these people that the greatest adventure lies beyond life in this physical body, and that all of us have the opportunity to explore this world provided we take up the spiritual exercises of ECK and practice them faithfully. Only when we have learned the knack of leaving the physical consciousness to enter the higher states can we know that death is but a door to the universal worlds.

Those who become skilled in the practice of ECK will be happy people, for it is by crossing the bar of death that one meets his inner Master and learns the truth of what lies beyond. Those with this ability are taught to become masters of all inner planes, and at the death of the physical bodies of their loved ones, they are able to save them from fear, pain and torment by taking them across the bar of death to the higher spheres.

There is a vast difference between those who have been

initiated in ECKANKAR and those who have not, which shows up at the death of either. The initiated go into the heavenly worlds, but the uninitiated remain within the cycle of birth and death to reap the good or bad harvest of their deeds.

The seat of Soul in the waking state is located at a focus behind the two eyes, known variously to us as the Tisra Til, the third eye, or the tenth door, though it is perhaps most commonly referred to as the spiritual eye. To travel in the subtle, spiritual worlds, the mind and Soul must first be collected and our attention fixed on this spot. It is the window between the physical and spiritual worlds.

Sometimes the thousand currents of spiritual forces in the astral plane, which gives energy to and supports our physical plane, are called the thousand petaled lotus, or the thousand headed serpent. But to those who have not developed their spiritual eye these forces may appear to be a single, spiritual flame. A pale, outer manifestation of this still exists in churches and temples where candles burn in imitation of the astral flame. The ringing of bells in places of worship is also a copy of the transcendental bell that represents the sound of the astral plane.

Man is the microcosm of the vast macrocosm comprising all of creation. As the greater consciousness seeps into the smaller consciousness via whatever opening it may have, so does the universal penetrate the personal. And, when the latter is hardened or filled with negative power, it must be opened in some manner that will allow the macrocosm to fill it with spiritual forces.

There is another aspect, however, which interests us even more. This is the inner mystic experience brought on by the movement of Soul. As we read about the experiences of those who have left their human state of consciousness and ascended into higher states, we learn that it is possible for most persons to have similar experiences.

These higher states, the true spiritual planes above the Soul world, are beyond the duality of the physical. Here we do not find good and evil, ugliness and beauty. All things

35

are indivisible, all-comprehending and all transcending. Realization of the God State is not a neutral or indifferent state. It is the combination of all ecstasy, knowledge, and love in the purest and most concentrated essence.

Once we have transcended all planes and entered into the true God world we discover Its illumination and divine consciousness in everything. Within the diversity of physical and psychic phenomena we discover this true, hidden unity, this singular part of God working in all things. We now know and see the God force in everything. By this time, however, we have gone beyond all desires, and our deeds are performed without any desire for the personal gains. Therefore, we need not go to great mountain tops, into caves, nor into the jungle to give up desire.

During a Soul's travel in the upper worlds it experiences truths beyond the intellectual grasp of man. When we try to use words to describe these experiences, however, anyone who has not known Soul Travel will find what seems, to him, to be great contradictions. There are no contradictions in these truths, but because they are truths revealed at different levels of consciousness, they appear to be so.

Absolute Truth is known only in the heart of the SUGMAD. But how many of us will ever reach this level of pure reality? The higher we go the truer is our view of God. The truths of any individual plane remain forever true for that plane, but these truths are always superseded by the truths of the higher planes. Truth, therefore, is relative on each plane to the ultimate Reality.

One question always comes up with every neophyte on the path of ECK. Could he do better with Soul Travel by learning self-hypnotism? The answer is negative. The work of ECK involves, as said before, fixing the attention on some inner point within ourselves. Now, we know that concentration is required in hypnotism, clairvoyance and other forms of occult practices, but these practices do not yield any spiritual unfoldment, nor even any spiritual knowledge. They are merely off-shoots of ECK.

The graduated scales of truth mentioned above are often

the downfall of many seekers after God. This is true of the various religions of the world. The spiritualists, for example, establish their heaven in the astral world. It is called the Summerland, and most followers of this movement go no further than that when they die. Similarly, the Christian religion has established its heaven on the fourth, or mental plane, where most of its followers dwell in a place called Paradise after they leave this world. None of them, not even the great saints, have scarcely traveled beyond this particular abode.

On closer examination, the fourth plane appears to be the heaven for all religions. The followers of Judaism, Islamism, Buddhism, Taoism, Bahaiism, Jainism, Shintoism, Sikkhism and Mithraism, to name but a few, adopt this plane of existence after quitting their physical bodies.

An important thing to remember at this point is that when any master or founder of a religion leaves this world, that religious body loses its divine spark. This is because the founding master acts as the polarity between his own followers and God. In a manner of speaking, he is God manifested on Earth. Without him there is no linkup between the Supreme Power and the remaining disciples.

In the case of true religious groups we find that when a master leaves his bodily form he no longer has anything to do with the world of physical matter. Generally he is succeeded by another, and those who are ready to follow the new master will go to him. In the case of ECK, however, it matters little whether one's Master has gone beyond or not. The ECK Master is always ready to serve whoever wishes to follow him into the world beyond.

When an individual develops some sort of religion through priests, creeds and organizations, it is hardly more than an outer form. Few who follow such a path will find the way to enter into the kingdom of heaven as taught by all ECK Masters. Only the living ECK Master has the key to the secret kingdoms.

We must sacrifice the world and our gross self before we can have a glimpse of the lofty Truth and Absolute Reality.

But this supreme sacrifice is not the renunciation of physical life as we have lived it, as it is so often misconstrued. It is the renunciation of the mind and its hold upon us. Those who are wordly minded are seldom able to perform these transcendent travels to other planes.

Before we can experience Soul Travel we must be purified. To do so we must uplift ourselves through association with the Master, and through reading and listening to his discourses. Conventional religions do not require this of their practitioners, but satisfy only those who look upon spiritual inquiry as a secondary thing to the life they live daily.

Upon examination we find three types of consciousness. First is sound sleep, in which there is no awareness or consciousness of anything. This is lowest on the scale, and what we call death consciousness. Animals often use it when attacked by larger and stronger animals. We ourselves are guilty of this, on occasion. When we wish to avoid certain elements of life we will often fall into this state of unconsciousness.

The second type of consciousness is dream consciousness, in which we have vague awareness. During this dream state everything is disjointed and disorderly, and when we awaken we are commonly unaware of what has taken place. It is usually characterized by the absence of any control over the will.

Consciousness becomes clearer in the waking state. In this condition we find our experiences are consistent and our perceptions clearer. We know what our situation may be, though our knowledge is based upon appearances. But, in accordance with the spiritual reality, we are still without conception of Truth. We are only working with the intellect, which is the highest faculty on this plane but also very unreliable.

The next ascending step is the immortal state. Once we have taken this step we have consciousness of the higher planes, where all things are subtle and Truth is the Ultimate Reality. At this stage the brain and the physical organs cease to operate, even as they do in sleep or a trance. The true self takes over, and only by our spiritual senses do we function within these worlds. This final step is gained only by Soul Travel.

There are likewise three divisions in the whole of creation. These are: the material worlds, the spirito-material worlds, and the pure spiritual regions.

The material universe, called the Pinda, consists of six planes of subtle matter. These planes constitute the psychic chakras that are so well known in the yoga philosophy. Unfortunately, these have been mixed up and hashed over by so many writers with only second hand knowledge of the Oriental religions that we scarcely know anything about this system. For our information, however, these six planes or chakras are the six nerve ganglions in the spine corresponding with the psychic centers of the lower universe.

The lowest of these is the Adhar Chakra. It is the four-petaled lotus, centered at the rectum and light red in color. It is the seat of the Earth element, and the first stage of the yogis. The word to be used here is "Kaling."

Next is the Swadhishthan Chakra. It is focused at the reproductive organs and represents the creative powers. It is the Water element and the second stage of yoga. The word repeated here is "Onkar." It is within the Swadhishthan Chakra that the Kundalini lies wrapped in sleep, waiting for the right concentration to arouse it. The practice to control this force is called Kundalini Yoga, and the light for this center is yellowish. It is also known as the six-petaled lotus.

The third center is called the Manipurak Chakra, or the eight-petaled lotus. Here the light is blue, and it is the seat of the Fire element. It is located opposite the navel in the spinal cord, and it represents the sustaining and nourishing power. The Manipurak Chakra is the third state in the practice of yoga, and the word repeated is "Hiring."

Fourth is the Anahag Chakra, which is the twelve-petaled lotus. The Anahag Chakra is focused on the heart center and represents the destructive power. It is also the breath center and the seat of the Air element. The light in this fourth stage of yoga is whitish, and the word to be repeated here is "Sohang."

39

Fifth is the Vishudha Chakra, which is the sixteen-petaled lotus. It is concentrated at the throat and is the seat of the Ether element. The color here is purple and the word the yogis use for repetition is "Shring" or "Ashtang."

The sixth plane is represented by the Dodal Chakra. It is the two-petaled lotus, and is black and white in color. It is located behind the two eyes and is the sixth stage of the yogis. The Dodal Chakra is ruled by the Mind element, and is opened by a repetition of the word "Aum."

The sixth chakra is the seat of Soul in the waking state. Its resting place is the third eye or the Tisra Til, as mentioned earlier, and it is above the six centers of material creation. It is from this place of rest that the chela must come forth in his Atma Sarup [Soul body] to meet the awaiting Master and travel with him in the higher worlds. The word here is, "HU".

Those who are on the path of ECK never go below this chakra. They know that for real spiritual experience they must ascend from the Tisra Til into the planes of pure spirit. Here is the world of the gods, where heroes of myth and legend live. They are not there to be worshipped, though, they are there to render service unto the chela. Brahm, Vishnu, and others must serve him, for he is higher than any and they are, in a manner of speaking, servants of Soul.

Here Soul, in the company of the Master, travels across the starry sky to the moon worlds, and from these to the lightning worlds, which the Vedanta religionists believe is the true heaven of bliss and joy. But past all this travel Soul and Master, to the first plane we call the astral. And, beyond this It goes through the causal and mental planes to the Soul plane, where begin the worlds of pure spirit.

Above the spiritual eye is the last subtle opening for Soul to leave the body without descending to the spirito-material chakras. This is called the Crown Chakra by the yogis. Some say it is the Sushamma and others call it the thousand-petaled lotus. But it is the last place for Soul to leave the body, and the easiest place to succeed with Soul Travel.

No man can enter into the heavenly spheres with his mind on things of the objective world; neither can he have any experience with God should his thoughts be with anything on the astral, causal or mental planes. We must close the nine doors of the objective world and concentrate upon the tenth or eleventh door.

The nine doors of the outer worlds are: the two eyes, two ears, two nostrils, the mouth, the sex organs and the rectum. These are the openings, or doors, in the body which can hold communication with the external world. When one practices the spiritual exercises of ECK, all attention must be withdrawn from these lower doors and placed upon the spiritual eye.

When all the outer world has been closed out, and even in the inner world of our thoughts our attention is fixed unwaveringly at the Tisra Til, then we are ready to step across the invisible veil between the objective and subjective worlds. We should lose all feeling and sensation of the existence of the body.

This point at the root of the nose, the spiritual eye, is the tenth door of the body through which Soul passes into the worlds beyond. This is the subtle door that must be opened to let us enter into the worlds of the invisible, which is the realm of God.

We look out through this door at the other worlds like a child who stays by a window watching the birds in the garden. His longing and hope to get through the window and play in the garden is magnified by his own imagination of what pleasures await him outside. We must apply this same principle in Soul Travel. We must desire to reach the inner worlds and imagine the enjoyment we will have in each.

When Soul passes through the spiritual window it enters first into the astral world, which is a much finer universe than the one in which the body lives. We cannot see this world with physical eyes, but instead we view everything on this plane with astral senses. This is true also of every higher plane we pass into.

41

The chela proceeds through sub-planes known as the "sun-worlds," the "moon-worlds," and finally into the "lightning worlds," which constitute the beginning of the pure astral worlds. This is conceived by many yogis to be the supreme heavenly world, and Niranjan, the ruler of this world, is likewise considered to be the Supreme Being. Many religions regard this world as the supreme heaven, because they do not know any better.

Between the sun-worlds and the moon-worlds there exists a zone of the pure astral plane called the Ashta-dal-Kanwal. When the chela enters this zone his whole life changes. Here he meets with the Master in his Nuri Sarup, or Light Form. His Master will appear just as he does in physical life, except now his body is illuminated brilliantly. The chela is received with much joy and from this moment on they are never separated through their journey to still higher regions.

Up until this time most of the chela's success with Soul Travel has been small. Now, however, there is a change. No longer does he need to sit performing the spiritual exercises and repeating the Zikar, for now he can enjoy the presence of the Master constantly. The perfect vision of the Master is much more effective than the Zikar for concentration. This phenomenon is called the Dhyana, when the very sight of the Master inspires tremendous affection.

It is now that the Sound Current will make contact with the chela in its greatest manner. The chela will find himself listening to it with intensity and being delightfully absorbed in it. From then onward his progress will be steady and accelerated. The Dhyana and the Sound Current, or Bani, as it is more commonly called, go together. Both are interlaced into one another until it is almost impossible to separate them.

When we go beyond the spirito-material planes we enter into the true spiritual worlds that comprise the heart of God. Only by the use of ECK can we take the straight road to this absolute kingdom. All other practices leave us in the lower worlds because the vehicle they use is not purely spiritual.

The ECK makes use of a true spiritual entity, and consequently gets us access into the pure spiritual regions. Whoever is properly initiated into the mysteries of ECK by a perfect adept may easily scale spiritual heights that are inaccessible to those who follow any other path to God.

All religions regard reality from their own viewpoint and therefore they frequently end up with a one-sided look. This is because none of them are free of maya, or the negative forces. When we deal with negative we find that we are really dealing with Kal, the personification of negative. And maya is, of course, the veil of illusion.

The entire Pinda universe is a huge prison with many rooms and cells. Our warden is Kal, or Kal Niranjan. But our true home is in the Sach Khand, our name for the secret kingdom of God.

Kal does not want to let any of his subjects be free to enter the spiritual worlds, nor does he want us to travel in our Light bodies towards God-Realization. Kal makes us believe that things are going to be better in this world by conjuring up prophets and moral, social and political reformers who continually attempt to set the world right.

But these are the agents of Kal. They act only with its power and only make their reforms within prison walls. None of them can tell us our real destiny is in the Sach Khand for they themselves are unaware of it. The ECK Masters, on the other hand, come from outside this prison to liberate all Souls from the Kal's possession forever. It is with the help and grace of these Masters that we leave this dark land of illusion and begin the journey homeward again.

Despite all the comforts provided by Kal we cannot leave his world for those higher until the Master releases us and takes every Soul away from it. Until this is done the cycle goes on in Kal's dominion, and Souls living there have no true peace. An ECK Master will not teach us how to improve this world, even as the social and political reformers try, but he will wisely teach us how to leave it by going out of the physical state and into the heavenly.

From time to time incarnations of the gods appear again in this world to re-establish righteousness, to protect the good and destroy the wicked. But their reforms, like those of the

43

prophets who occasionally reappear, are all in the sphere of morality. None of them take us to the Absolute Reality.

These incarnations are known to us as the saviours. Many of them, like Jesus, Krishna and Zoroaster, have been the founders of world religions. Yet none of them are able to take us into our true home with the Supreme Deity. The history of this planet is filled with the incarnations of prophets, saviours and reformers who have tried to straighten out the world.

But above all these we find that the ECK Masters are the true agents of God, and that they come from the heart of the Divinity. They are merciful and filled with compassion for those trapped in the meshes of the Kal power. They are free from the law of Kal that binds most Souls to the prison of Earth. They are not concerned with good or evil or the laws of karma, but with the totality of God. They are true God-men who come to show us how to transcend the morality and iron shackles of these lower worlds.

Kal and his chief manifestation—maya, or illusion—have in their power all men, angels, gods, magicians, priests, cults, yogis, mahatmas, sages, mursheeds, and maharishis. Only the Sat-Guru and the Vi-Guru are agents of the Purushottama, the supreme creative energy. This energy is known as spiritual power.

Self-realization followers who take much of their teachings from the yoga of Patanjali put immense faith in the three gunas: sattva, rajas and tamas—light, motion and darkness. But these are aspects of the universal mind power, and proof of the workings of Kal. As followers of ECK we must go beyond all things of the lower worlds, which includes mind, and be a part of the realm of God.

The ECK Masters live in sublime humility, remaining practically unknown to the masses, who consider ordinary prophets, reformers and mystics to be the higher beings. Social and political reformers make great names for themselves in this world, and become gods for the people. But the Masters are hardly ever either recognized or followed, except by a few.

There are four classes of students on the path of ECK-ANKAR:

(1) Those who read and talk about the discourses but do not practice the spiritual exercises. They expect instant success with scarcely any effort. These people are leaners, and want everything to be done for them, instead of having to do something for themselves. This, is however, the stage of their spiritual growth, and perhaps they should not be in the study of ECK.

(2) Those who study the discourses and listen to the Master but, not being completely successful, become restless and take up the study of other works. These may get a glimpse of the transcendent realms but they are never at home in them.

(3) Those who obey the Master and follow him completely, but do not have the spiritual unfoldment to get into the heart of the secret kingdom. They are faithful and they try, but the Master will not force their unfoldment, as such action would only ultimately slow their progress.

(4) Those who have attained the freedom to travel into the absolute center of God, and have made their permanent home there.

Here are developments one can more readily recognize in people. These are: (1) Those who talk about God and the divine wisdom without having attained either by inner enlightenment. These people have many questions and want to have meetings with other persons. (2) Those who do the spiritual exercises of ECK with zeal and earnestness, puting their hearts and interest into the works. This path brings to those who follow it a spiritual realization of God. (3) Those who have reached the stage of ultimate Truth and have the ability to dwell in the higher planes. This is the ultimate goal of ECK. It is attained only after one has completed the second stage of development and has made his home in the subtle spiritual realms. Those in ECK who have reached this position are known as the ECKshar, or the Christ

Consciousness, for they live in the ethereal regions of God. They have become the ECK and will adopt a body only during the hours of the day when they have to deal with the people of this physical universe. Those who travel the path of ECK must be bold and adventurous. The hardships are great until the true worlds are entered. But in order to reach this higher level of spiritual consciousness each Soul is required to go through the trial of fire and water in the inner worlds. As the Acolyte treads the path of ECK his old concepts of God die within, and a new understanding comes into his life. He dies to his old life and is reborn to the new.

The Mahanta looks upon all individuals as perfect Souls who have not recognized their true selves. It is his responsibility to help each Soul to both regain himself and learn to take advantage of the opportunity to reach heaven again. The Mahanta flatly states that the concepts of orthodox religion are wrong, that we do not have to wait for the death of the physical body to re-enter heaven. And, not only can we do it daily, but we can also dwell there while retaining use of the body on Earth.

Therefore, those following the path of ECK are not interested in the metaphysics of religions, nor the philosophies of man. Their attention is riveted on the higher worlds, for they know that anyone who desires it can obtain Jivan Mukti, or salvation here and now.

Those immersed in world religions say this cannot be done, but the ECK Masters assure us that the opportunity is always awaiting those truly interested in trying to obtain this supreme goal. Unless we find the SUGMAD now, in this life, and reach those subtle spiritual planes while still living in the physical body, what guarantees the religionists' claim that we can do so following physical death?

Therefore, we should not place all our hopes in receiving salvation after death, but continue to search here for the transcendental secrets, and in this life dwell in the knowledge of the Ultimate Reality. We should understand that the religions, philosophies and creeds of this world represent little more than death cults. Never does salvation occur here on

46

Earth, but always in some heavenly kingdom after death. Beliefs like these made it a common practice among the primitive Christians to seek death in any manner possible, that they might enter into their promised salvation. The Moslems were taught to believe in a delightful paradise where man was given all that he had missed in his earthly life.

Both liberation from this world and life in the secret kingdom of God are possible in this lifetime. It all depends upon ourselves.

CHAPTER FOUR

UNLOCKING THE KEY TO THE SPIRITUAL WORLDS

ECK cannot be resolved with any religion or philosophy at the mind level. It is always in conflict with the many teachings and preachings of this world. This is true and will always remain so because neither religions nor philosophies are able to go above the mental levels. Consequently, until one breaks through into the higher regions, this conflict is never resolved.

The ECK Master can lead the chela through this mental level provided he is allowed to do so. But as long as the chela does not accept the ECK teachings as truth there will always be within him the self-dissension that nothing is right. He will battle with himself, and fight against both the truth and the ECK Master, until he is completely exhausted.

When the chela reaches this state of utter mental and physical fatigue from chewing over points and arguing with others about spiritual matters, then he is apt to take one of two courses. He has come to the fork in the road. Here he must decide whether he wants to go to the left, thus quitting the path of ECK, or the right, which is accepting it fully.

Should he quit and take the left hand road, it would lead him into a state of confusion and floundering. As he tried to travel it, he would find his way beset with obstacles that he would have to overcome. In a very real sense, his state would be that of Christian in Pilgrim's Progress, who met with every means possible in the hands of the negative power to stop him from traveling the road to God.

Should he take the right hand path leading directly to God, he would find he must give up every preconceived notion in his life that had been formed since childhood. He would surrender himself to God. He would give up everything within himself and be guided by the mystical power of the ECK. Because of Its greater wisdom and Its understanding of the weaknesses and strengths of the individual chela, the ECK will take all who surrender to Its guidance into God-Realization.

This is the key to the spiritual worlds. One must surrender to the ECK and it will give us everything in life. None can deny this but many will argue the battle so fiercely against this method that they will appear to be driven out of their minds at times. The struggle between the mind powers and the ECK is very severe at times. It is more so in men than in women.

Now we have reached the heart of the problem of opening the way into the spiritual worlds, for frankly, metaphysics is all theory. It involves very little practice except on a mental level, and many times this amounts to hardly anything for those seeking the higher consciousness.

Repetition of words and phrases from sacred scriptures is good, for it opens the consciousness and allows the ECK to flow through. It also raises the vibrations of those who practice such methods. But there is a limit to this: the whole key lies in whether the individual practicing this method has the necessary awareness to be successful at it, or the patience to develop this awareness.

The subject of metaphysics creates a lot more problems than it solves, for those who teach the mind level religions are hindering their students rather than helping them. They give the student a lot of sophisticated data and drop it into his lap without saying anything more. This creates a barrier between the student and the point of surrender, and also fosters arguments with the master and other chelas on the mental levels.

I have said many times that every individual is on a different level in all departments of their lives. The Jeffersonian theory that all men are "created equal" is wrong. We do not all hold the same state of awareness for many reasons, the chief one being that in this life we are concerned with environmental awareness. This is true also, to a large extent, in the spiritual worlds. We do not hold the same spiritual environmental awareness as others do, but as I have often said, "Everyone is different. Therefore, I must give each one a different approach into the heart of God. Each of us must find his own way, but I will point out the way. I cannot give you God-Realization, but I can offer the opportunity to reach this stage of spiritual development."

It is in the nature of woman to surrender, and consequently more women than men will give up everything for the ECK. The life of a woman is usually governed by the invisible things of life, mainly love, while a man tends to be active and violent, to conquer, plunder and challenge. He is mostly concerned with life, and to him love is more or less an episode. He feels important when physical and spiritual love are united within him, that is, when he is conscious of his masculinity in association with the creative powers. To man this is the true definition of living in the spiritual heights.

The spiritual key we are about to discuss is a paradox within this physical universe. When we consider it we must remember one thing: that spiritual virtues do not reign in this world except by strong personalities. Sometimes these people are unsuccessful at exerting their positive influence in a world ruled by negative forces. Therefore, it is usually the ECK Master who is able to overcome any manifestations of the Kal power and rule in its stead.

The key itself lies in the element of non-attachment. We know that in this physical universe violence begets violence, but kindness and other spiritual virtues will not always beget spiritual virtues. This is because each is an aspect of the higher law. The same holds true for love, for love of itself will not beget love.

To understand this, take a look at the saviours of the world. Jesus Christ, for example, was not universally loved by the peoples of His day. He was, in fact, a very hated figure, because he was stirring up too much trouble with the Romans and upsetting the social structure of the Jews. This is indeed an example of love begetting hatred. It all comes back to one thing, and that is that we are living in a negative world, which very few people realize.

51

Too many are being told that love will get them everything in this life, which is not exactly true. While this is an ideal way of living, at the same time it is not very practical. I am not saying that a person should live a life of distrust and hatred, but I do think we must realize that love is not the way. Non-attachment is the only real key to living in this physical universe. If we learn this, our lessons are completed and our karmic burden will pass away.

When a person enters into this life to study ECK he must remember that his ideal is freedom, and not love so much as non-attachment. This is the Vairag state, in which we are detached from worldly desires and, in particular, a mental love of the world. This does not imply asceticism, which is to reject all material things and live in a state of non-being—like a vegetable—and think only of God.

This is the key to the spiritual worlds. This is what unlocks the door and gives us the entry into the kingdom of God and the glories of heaven. The state of successful detachment from a love of worldly things is what the ECK Masters have reached. They are members of the ancient Order of Vairagi Masters, and if any of them need to live here in the physical realm they can accept social responsibility while at the same time remaining detached from all things.

This is a difficult state to reach, but when one does he becomes free of all material life. He has successfully achieved that level of spiritual development so many are striving to reach. It will take others longer, according to their level of spiritual development. We enter into the path of ECK knowing that life gives us what we take from it. If we take from it detachment or spiritual unfoldment, then all will go well and the key is ours to unlock the heavenly kingdom.

Thus the ECK is not an idea image, but an ideal one. We are always unfolding and striving to enter into this image of idealism, and it is for this reason that nobody nor anything—be it in this material world or in the spirit worlds—can defeat one who is submerged in the ECK. The ECK takes care of Its own, protects and loves us with Its omniscience, omnipotence and omnipresence. It acts as an ideal and brings all Its forces into play against those who try to take advantage of or harm Its followers.

It is for this reason that the ECK Master is so important. He is the true channel for the ECK within this world and like all other men on this physical plane, he consists of an amortal physical body and an immortal body. This amortal body is subject to the laws of nature and must function accordingly. It must be fed, washed, and taken care of so that the best use can be made of it.

The ECK Master uses this physical vehicle to give his message to the world. It forms the outer messenger and serves those who are seeking the true path to God. The physical body is, in fact, the instrument of the ECK, serving Its purpose in this world. And, interestingly, it is not immune to any of the ailments that attack us upon the physical plane.

Many people believe that a spiritual master is free from all harm, disease, and the problems that beset the rest of humanity. But this is in no way true. If it were so, then many of the masters would not have been martyred, nor died of disease, nor been killed while preaching the message of God. Few of the saints died free from violence. Ramakrishna left his physical body due to cancer of the throat; Krishna, the Christ of India, was killed by his enemies when they tied him to a tree and shot arrows through his body.

Of course, many ECK Masters have escaped this kind of treatment. This is because they practiced the spiritual exercises of ECKANKAR which enabled them to reach a higher level of life. This higher level in turn freed them from the harm inherent upon this physical plane. It is for this reason that we say the ECK protects and gives Its cloak of guardianship over all Its followers. Once we have achieved any degree of spiritual development in ECK It takes over our lives and guides us through the obstacles of the lower worlds with a deftness that defeats all the negative forces at work against us.

The ECK Master is the inner, spiritual form. He takes care of all chelas who are under his guidance. This inner

53

form is the spark of divinity, the original Cause of all that there is. The Master has the same three attributes as the supreme SUGMAD: 1.) God awareness, 2.) realization of the Master or the great channel, and 3.) realization of the ECK Itself.

Soul builds and controls the physical body by these attributes. This creative process depends upon the spiritual unfoldment of Soul and the degree of its awakened consciousness, and explains why each man is different from another man. This is also in accord with the law of spiritual evolution, which presupposes inequality in all things and beings and their continued effort for self-improvement in life.

Thus we find three characteristics of the human state of being in the physical body of man. The first of these is inertia. No material substance or body is activated or moved by itself unless an inner force or an outer one causes this motion or activity. Usually it is the inner force that moves the body.

The second characteristic is disintegration. Every form or body, be it plant, animal, or the physical body of man, is in a constant struggle to liberate itself from the control of Soul, or the spiritual entity responsible for its creation. This conflict between the ECK and matter manifests as life.

The physical body will exist on the plane of its natural habitation as long as Soul is able to control it and direct it toward useful activities and purposes in life. Under these conditions the ECK Masters are able to maintain control over their bodies for indefinite periods of time, even for centuries.

The very moment this control Soul has over body starts to diminish to the point that it loses its supremacy over matter, the body, through its latent characteristic of disintegration, will start breaking down until death ends the physical life of this person.

The third characteristic of matter is transformation. When the physical embodiment is broken down into its primordial elements and then revitalized by the force of the negative power—or nature—these elements will be utilized again in accordance with the laws of ECK by another Soul.

Soul takes the primordial elements and rebuilds a new physical body to suit Its own needs and to continue Its purpose of physical life on Earth. The process of the ECK acting upon matter in this manner was started at the beginning of time in this physical universe, and will continue through all the yugas, known as the Day of God in His creation. The yugas are based on the law of spiritual evolution, and continue to the end of time, which is known correspondingly as the Night of God.

Then physical matter and all beings with both their earned experiences and developed Soul consciousness return to the heavenly worlds. When the physical universes are destroyed man will be stripped of his material bodies and pulled up into the higher regions to rest until a new physical universe is again established. Then, if any individual Soul has to return to accumulate more experience or complete his unfoldment, a place is made ready for him.

This is what we know as the ebb and tide of divine consciousness in matter within the cosmic ECK. This cycle serves each Soul in its journey along the path to God, for Self-Realization is a state of consciousness achieved through spiritual unfoldment in the media of matter. Through this process we reach an understanding of how the ECK forces work throughout the cosmos. A complete understanding will also give purpose to, and solve the mystery of, creation in eternity by the divine SUGMAD.

The detached state is by far the most important step a chela can take in preparing himself for the great spiritual works. Everyone who comes to the ECK must be duly and truly prepared and well qualified before he can receive initiation. If he is not ready it will do him little good to attempt entrance into this state whereby he can expect to receive secret instructions from the inner Master.

He must be able to make his own way in life—to earn his own keep and not live off another. Whatever a person has been in the past is now of no consequence. Whether he has been a hardened criminal or an individual with loose

55

morals, once he enters the path of ECKANKAR, it is his attitude and not his past deeds that count.

The first step in ECKANKAR is the Viveka, or right discrimination. The chela must learn to discriminate between what will be good for his spiritual advancement and what would be wasting his time. Man being what he is, the supreme consciousness is often wasted, for man has no recognition of his own true self. He is the ECK, like the Master, but he does not as yet recognize his full potential.

Until the chela sees everything in this world as the working of the SUGMAD, every variety of evil contained in Kal's bag of tricks will continue to hold him back. But eventually the chela will arrive at the state referred to in the Shariyat-Ki-Sugmad when it stated that, "All is one, but every sage will have a different name for it."

What is being specifically referred to here is love, for love is the adhesive force that holds everything together. It is the love of God, then, that keeps the universes from becoming unglued. This is known as the doctrine of universal unity. When we speak of it we are dealing directly with the heart of God.

Once we recognize that all things are governed by this great law of love we can proceed along the path without serious interference from that negative bag of tricks. When we discover that we are safely beyond the reach of the Kal influence we have reached the state of recognition Moses experienced when standing before the burning bush. "I Am That I Am!" he heard it say. Only now we have arrived at the point wherein it can be said, "I Am This!"

In the Indian philosophy it is stated differently, as, "Thou Art That!" This is not quite true, though, for it implies something outside of ourselves speaking the words. A similar expression is also found in another part of the Sanskrit writings stating, "I Am That!" This again, however, refers to something outside ourselves.

The true meaning of all these sacred expressions is "This I Am!" This means that the individuality within the person is able to separate itself and become its own. At the same time, however, it implies an understanding that all things are of the same divine essence, and that each of us is the ECK.

Therefore there is no difference between the supreme ECK and each individual Soul. All are part of the ECK Itself. We are all expressing the divine Cause in every act of our daily lives. We are not God, nor are we any part of the Deity, as claimed by the Hindus. What we are is a part of the cosmic force called the ECK, and by both entering into It and taking part in It, we are one with the Allness of Life. It is here that the Indian teachers make their error, in mistaking the ECK for God. It is not God, but it is the essence of God. It is the part of Him that we know as Light and Sound.

We must remember always, though, that the more we enter into the ECK—the more we are a part of It—the more individualized Soul becomes. It enters into a state of freedom beyond any conception possible within this physical world. For this is the purpose of ECK: to preserve the individuality, which leads to complete liberty. And the kind of liberty offered by the ECK does not restrict itself to the limited political freedom offered by the Declaration of Independence and the Constitution of the United States.

There is such a vast difference between political and spiritual freedom that we in the human state of consciousness cannot even have the smallest amount of understanding about it. All freedom that comes via Soul is a revelation of the divine SUGMAD through Light and Sound. The state of supernatural grace to which we ascend (not that which descends upon us, as promised by the religionists) can be gained through the spiritual exercises of ECK.

The initiate knows this, for he gains certain spontaneous experiences from the practices given him via personal instruction from the ECK Master at the time of initiation. And, while studying under the Master, the initiate reaches even higher levels of experience.

Furthermore, I wish to state at this time that the term "bilocation," which is the ability to be in two places at the same time, is no longer in the vocabulary of ECK. This word has been dropped from our terminology because it sounds too much like astral projection. The expression "Soul Travel" is used instead, as it gives more depth and breadth to the teachings of ECK.

Perhaps at this point it would be best to clarify the definitions of ECKANKAR and ECK for all who follow this path. These definitions should serve as springboards in answer to any future questions.

ECKANKAR: The ancient science of Soul Travel. Projection of the inner consciousness, which travels through the lower states until it ascends into the ecstatic states. Here the subject feels he possesses an awareness of the religious experience of being. This awareness is achieved through a series of spiritual exercises known only to the followers of this science.

ECK: The science of Total Awareness that grows out of the experiences of Soul Travel. The subject gains this state of religious awareness at his own volition, via the spiritual exercises of ECKANKAR. The latter is correlated only with the movement of the inner consciousness—Soul—within the regions of time and space. The ECK goes above these regions, beyond time and space, where all is omniscient, omnipresent and omnipotent. Hence the term, Total Awareness.

This Total Awareness is the key we use to enter the kingdom of God. It is a channel, a tunnel, or what other groups call the Christ Consciousness. This state, known to us as the ECKshar, is what we all must come to and go through to become the ECK. This spiritual state leads to a perfected consciousness from which we are able to reach the esoteric heights. We must spiritualize the mind and body by saturating ourselves with the spiritual ideal.

ECK must therefore come first in the life of every initiate. And It will demand more and more of the individual until It has all of him. The person will suffer, cry, complain, and resist all the changes the ECK is making within him, but it is a useless struggle. The sooner he ceases to fight against any changes, the sooner he gains true freedom.

The ECK will break down all the prejudice, intolerance, possessiveness, vanity, craving for drugs and alcohol, laziness, anger, unkindness, faultfinding, attachment, bigotry, and impatience, all of which are listed as attributes of Kal.

The ECK will tear out the influence of the Kal power and put in its place the spiritual nature of Itself. It will establish the God influence in our lives, whereby we become an instrument of the Divine Power. As such we work within this world, uplifting others and putting their feet on the path of ECK. It will reward us for being obedient to Its will by guiding our lives into the proper channels. It will take care of our physical welfare as well as our spiritual endeavors by taking us into the heart of God. There the eternal joys are ours.

Principally It gives us individuality and freedom for, as stated previously, the whole purpose of ECK is the preservation of individuality. This state of freedom, however, is never understood by anyone living within the physical senses. This freedom has nothing to do with economics and the physical successes of life, for even the poorest of men can live in Its state of being completely free.

I have often told my chelas: "I will stretch you so far that it will seem to you that you are a rubber band. It will hurt at times, but if you will stay with me then you will one day look back and wonder if you are the same person who started out with me."

We are working to reach a state of devotion and service. The ECK Master is an inspiring example to anyone who wishes to make this first step on the path to God. This method is called the way of discipleship, for if one tries to live and think like the ECK Master he will consequently discipline himself, that the true spiritual works may enter into his life.

The very core and substance of the teachings of ECK is to love the SUGMAD and your fellowman. If one does not have this love he is only wasting his time in trying to approach the Master. The major test in everyman's life when he desires to become a chela is whether or not he has a love for all that lives. This is the universal love that binds the universe.

The ECK Master loves all chelas and all life despite the

59

love that a chela has only for himself. This is the mark of the living ECK Master. He loves all things more than they would love him, and any man more than he loves his self-indulgences. This is a love that passes all human understanding.

Therefore, the chela must accept his share of the Master's love with an attitude of devotion and service. Never once should he waver or weaken in this love nor in his loyalty to the ideals of the ECK, for they are apparent in the Master's characteristics.

In the Bhagavad Gita, Krishna established ideals for the chela who has made the proper mental preparations to travel the path of God. He tells Arjuna the following things to do in order to lay a foundation for the spiritual life:

First, one should learn to endure the contacts of matter—heat and cold, pleasure and pain—for they come and go. They are not permanent. And, as Soul is always invulnerable, the wise never grieve for the dead or the living. Soul, which is the real self of every man, cannot be harmed either in life or in death, so there is no need to worry about what may happen to anyone. One must learn to take as equal either pleasure or pain, gain or loss, victory or defeat. The chela must learn to be above the opposites of life.

Krishna makes it clear that one must be concerned with the action, and never with the results or what it will bring. One should never be motivated by the results of any action, nor should he be attached to inaction. All the while he should be balanced evenly in success and failure.

The chela must be mentally stable, indifferent to anxiety, pains, anger, passion, fear. He must be without attachment. When one either reaches any one of these states, or deeply longs to enter into them, then he is ready to become a chela on the path of ECK. When he is worthy, the Master appears to greet him. Of all these, though, the most important step in the mental preparation of the chela is the Vairag.

Most people who take up these spiritual works do so after a long search through many books and movements. They have spent a great deal of time reading whole libraries on various subjects. But after awhile they learn that in modern times, neither belonging to a specific group nor studying under certain teachers can give man the ultimate way to resolve his problems and lead him to God.

When all else has failed we find that the ECK has always been there, awaiting the end of our weary search. Yet even after being accepted by the Master many chelas will still want to read every sort of book, belong to three or four different religious movements, take discourses from several others, and try to absorb everything they can get their hands upon. This is somewhat of a habit, but it comes mostly from the desire to clarify one's own thinking on spiritual matters.

This, too, is the basic reason why so many seekers on the path try to get themselves close to a Master. They only want to ask questions to get their own thinking straightened out, but as Sudar Singh, the great ECK Master, once replied to a large number of questions asked of him, "What is there to say? Have faith, believe in God."

The chela seeking to enter the works of ECK should first have a clear understanding of what It is and what the ideals of the ECK Masters are, insofar as he can on his level of spiritual understanding. These ideals, of course, are of far greater value than any rules or principles.

If the chela has accepted what he has found in his study of the works and has become filled with the ideals of the ECK Masters, then his next step is the Vairag. The Vairag is, as mentioned before, the detachment of one's self from the outer world. The chela simply removes his thoughts from the love of the world and from worldly desires. This should not be confused with asceticism, for in ECK we think more in terms of giving up the desire for the external things rather than the things themselves.

One does not detach himself from the world, leaving his family, his social responsibilities and his work. Rather, the Vairag means that we must detach ourselves in our innermost feelings from interest in the things of our everyday lives. We do not cease to identify ourselves with our environment or possessions, instead we give up our affection for them.

They are simply no longer the essence of our life and thought, and in this way we are independent of them.

This still applies to those close to the chela, such as his family. But it does not mean that he cannot love them. Instead, he now has more control over it than before, which means he can maintain his own freedom. This is the heart of the matter. This is the key to the spiritual worlds. If the chela truly practices this his life will never be injured by physical losses.

The material world and all the people within it belong, as Shakespeare declared, to "the passing show." And, if all that man may take with him when he leaves this world are his inner possessions, then why should they not be the best, the highest in spiritual experiences? All physical things are but a momentary interest in life, they are not his own, and his attachment to them is temporary. They are like a loan to us, for we must have them and use them here in this life.

The chela who has gained the quality of non-attachment must not assume an attitude of self-righteousness. This would defeat his aim in life and nullify the progress of his spiritual unfoldment. He must keep vanity away from his mental door and be humble in the presence of all. The greatest mark of anyone who has attained the higher levels of spirituality is humility. The chela realizes that he is in the awed presence of some supernatural force, and he knows that he must bow to it.

We must avoid bondage to the world and its objects of sensual desire, for when we want to possess something we enter into slavery. We must never look for rewards, for when we do we become bound to these rewards, and karma is our master. We must have no concern for the rewards of our actions. We must reach the state of mind in which we are like the sun, which shines upon all without asking anything in return.

This is how the chelas should regard the Master, for he is the ideal. He gives his love to all alike and never asks anything for it in return. Soul lives by giving, and never by receiving. The paradox is that one gets most by giving most. Those in poverty are those who receive without giving.

When one gives without ever thinking of rewards he is in the first stage of immortality. The ECK Masters did not reach their high state by fleeing from pain, or from finding comfort or sensual pleasures. Detachment from worldly things in a serene manner is the last step before entering the door to complete freedom. When one has reached this stage of spiritual unfoldment he will find that his humility grows, and the blame formerly put upon others is only a reflection of his own faults. This is the highest ideal that he can reach, therefore, he is always in the act of self-purification instead of trying to reform others.

This is the true detachment, the true Vairag. For we must learn that it is typical of human consciousness to quickly place the blame of faults and problems in another direction than our own door. The real trouble of course, lies within ourselves. Once we have learned this we quickly realize the law that states: "One's true self includes the whole of life, and the wrongs of others are their own wrongs."

What does this mean? It means that we have no problems that are not the problems of the entire human race. We cannot, therefore, consider the ECK Master as an ordinary human person, like the rest of us, for upon his shoulders fall the problems of the whole world. He is the singular one who is responsible for all the things that go on within the universes of God. This sounds very strange but it is true.

One must look to the ECK Master, then, for he is not only bearing the errors and mistakes of your past lives, but he is trying to get each individual to realize his own responsibility for his thoughts and actions. Once this realization is reached the individual will be able to lift the burden from himself and be of assistance to others. Until he does, though, it will be the responsibility of the Master to get him into the heavenly worlds, where he may learn the best way for himself.

Few realize it, but this is the reason for world karma and racial karma. It is also why no ECK Master will attempt to change or resolve the karma of the human race. The human race comprises the World Soul, and by trying to resolve its karma, the Master would only take on more. As it stands he also refuses to step in and relieve the world of its earned debt. The human race must take on its own responsibility for its debt, and work it out. This will be possible in approximately thirteen million years, at which time the Earth will come to an end in this universe.

The ECK Master is the true teacher for all the universe, including every planet, star and constellation. He is responsible for the works of ECK on every plane, in every spiritual world, from the heart of God to the lowest of the physical universes. There are many study groups involved in ECK trying to unfold individually as well as collectively. Whether these study groups are on the planet Mars, in cities there, or within the cities and communities of the nations of this world, the Master is there with them, teaching, giving revelation to all who are seeking and wanting to find God through ECK.

He is able to give freedom to many now, through initiation. He can help them find the spiritual key because they are ready. Many others are not yet ready. They will have to take time to unfold to the level upon which they can receive the key of life through the Master.

Once the perfect state of the Vairag is reached one finds himself left without desire. This is the true secret of every great Master who has entered the heart of God. If one wants nothing he gains everything. But if one allows desire to run him, a battle is fought between Soul and mind that never lets one rest.

Desire is the offspring of the senses. When these senses want something their power overwhelms the mind and enslaves the Soul. From there the mind goes on creating karma, and becomes entangled in the net of Kal, the negative power. This is the purpose of Kal—to slyly entangle the mind and eventually take over Soul.

The terrible fight between the ECK and Kal in this world is often described in my lectures and writings. Man becomes the battlefield between these two forces, which in this world are somewhat equal in strength. He is torn asunder in their fight to establish supremacy over him.

If man fastens his attention upon something spiritual, some aspect of God, something that is imperishable, it will liberate him. But should he keep his mind on things of the material world — an attachment to his wealth, poverty, his job, family, or whatever it might be in these lower worlds—he will be bound to it.

Therefore we should have no attachment to anything. The desireless state is our salvation; it is our freedom and liberation from the material levels. When we become afraid that all is going to be taken from us, then we are letting ourselves be trapped in the Kal power.

While we are living in the human state we cannot allow ourselves to be pulled by the Kal into its negative trap. On this physical plane we live always within a dualistic consciousness that pulls us downward, while its opposite pulls us upward. We must therefore establish a desire in the opposite direction from the Kal. This is the crux, the secret of life. We must learn to be stronger in our desire for God.

Despite the teachings of Buddha, who was one of the first to succeed in establishing desire as the problem of man, few have ever reached the desireless state. But we know that there is only one way to establish ourselves in it and this is through the ECK, that marvelous Sound Current flowing out of the throne of God and touching all things within Its universes.

When we have consciously entered into this state all things become possible for us. The very key to the spiritual worlds is placed in our hands and we open the door to enter them. There is no other way except through the ECK Master, who places the key in our hands.

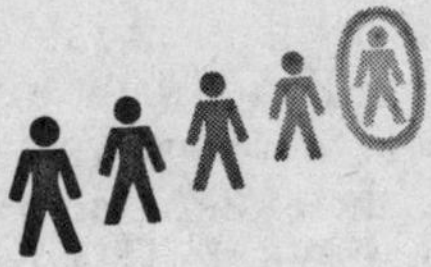

CHAPTER FIVE

THE CREATIVE TECHNIQUES

At the start of this chapter I want to point out that there is no reason to believe that the masses of people will ever take much interest in ECK, except when the whole social structure of a country is under attack or the world is falling to pieces. It is doubtful whether they even should, for the existing minor hubbub of metaphysics, spiritualism, orthodoxy, religions and cults would become extinct if the voice of ECK were added to the already present confusion.

So it is that in all this struggle and welter of living in the physical universe, the ECK Master must always contend with correcting the chelas' efforts. He is put into the position of having to say, "No, that is not right," whenever a chela starts to do something the wrong way. This is because the chela is not yet advanced enough to have spiritual knowledge of the right way to do things. Therefore, this world is always foreign to the ECK Adept, for he is continually at the opposite pole of the negative force. This force is out to destroy him, as it did all saviours and savants who have come here to give out Truth.

His interest is not in this world, as is that of the reformers and sociologists, who want to make justice for all in the physical plane. The ECK Master is interested only in the heavenly state. And, as this is where he wants all Souls to go, he must spend his time within the world of matter helping them to get out of it. He must show them that they can live in the beyond even before physical death takes away the body.

He does this through a series of creative exercises, called the spiritual exercises of ECK. These were instituted for the chela, that he may have a full, satisfactory knowledge that he is experiencing the subjective, or divine, adventure in the God worlds. We of ourselves can go no further than this, but leading the way is the ECK Master, who takes care of the flock following this secret path to heaven. He is concerned for the sinner and the lost, for even these are capable of taking the responsibility for themselves and following the Master's instructions to the last word.

I have said many times that what we are working with is states of consciousness and not projection of inner bodies, as so many people believe. The planes of the visible and invisible worlds should be thought of as states of consciousness. Therefore, movement from one plane to another is simply a matter of projection of consciousness, while here on the physical plane we must move about in the body, via planes, automobiles, trains and the like, not to mention simple leg-power.

What we are actually doing is moving the body from one physical place to another, but where different states exist. We are aware that there is a different state of consciousness existing in Athens from that in Salt Lake City, due to various factors that include race, geographical position, customs, and habits. Such examples exist all over the world. After we have traveled for a while, though, we find that there is something which gives us a common, conventional recognition, and that this goes with all races and all individuals. When we find something in common we soon discover that we are not far from our original state of consciousness, formed in our own community.

When we see this as true of our plane, we must begin to realize that each plane of existence has the same resemblance within its own sphere of influence. In a sense, the astral plane will be completely different to those visiting there from the physical, but once it is entered with any degree of regularity proof will be shown that this plane, as well as the causal and mental, are the phenomena of the mind stuff. This is true because the universal mind power rules the lower worlds. We know it mainly as the negative force, but all religions and cults think it to be the true God power.

We must realize that the negative force is controlled by Kal Niranjan, who is actually a part of the spiritual hier-

archy of God. He is stationed at the negative pole of creation
—at the top of the three worlds—and is the creator of the
spirito-material worlds.

This is why so many ancient rishis believed he was the
Supreme Creator, and why so many religionists today accept him as the highest of all, the divinely ultimate God.

In contrast with Kal Niranjan is the SUGMAD, true God
of the world and the positive power. IT rules the whole of
creation, from the positive pole to the end of all universes
of universes. It is a very significant fact that below the
positive pole no member of the spiritual hierarchy has the
power to create Souls. They do have creative powers, but none
to either create or destroy Souls.

It is very important to note here that all worlds of the Kal
force are created and run by the mechanics of time and
space. It is a universe of imperfection, but as long as we
are within it Soul does dwell in time and space and must
abide by the laws of the Kal. It is the duty of this negative
power to hold us here, and it is our duty to escape.

This is further reason for our interest in Soul Travel.
ECKANKAR, as stated previously, is the Ancient Science of
Soul Travel, and is concerned only with movement in time
and space. ECK, however, is the realization of God-consciousness, or Total Awareness, and is found in the upper
worlds. These worlds are above the fifth plane, and are
known as the worlds of pure spirit.

ECK is thus the thread, so fine as to be invisible yet so
strong as to be unbreakable, that binds together all beings
in all planes, all universes, throughout all time and beyond
all time into eternity. It is the thread that has woven the
history of this world and other worlds, binding events together, so that each generation can understand the past
karmic effects that will dominate its present life.

The ECK comes out of the God center, that nameless and
inaccessible world. It flows out like a gigantic wave, carrying all Its power and all life upon Its breast to the outer-
most bounds of creation—which would be the negative pole
where Kal Niranjan rules. Then it flows back again to Its

original source, taking with It all Souls that are perfected and will become co-workers with God.

When the ECK enters into the region of the negative force It does so with such powerful effect that the result is as startling as a bolt of lightning. This is why so many persons become fearful of traveling beyond this worldly plane. Upon witnessing this strange phenomena just below the Soul plane, they often retreat into the physical state of consciousness and do not want to return to such awesome sights.

Then, too, the physical shock of the spiritual ECK entering into the magnetic field of the individual is likely to be felt with shattering impact. For here, again, the ECK is entering into the negative field which in part comprises an individual's makeup in the physical world.

When the ECK, the spiritual force, meets with the negative, the physical force, such as entering into the flesh, the resultant impact can shake the receiver badly. This occurs when an individual opens himself to the ECK force in some manner; for example, through reading too much, through attempts at meditation, or through spiritual exercises he has either read about or had laid down for him by his spiritual director. Frankly, there is great danger in undergoing instructions from books bought on open shelves or taken from any school or city library.

It is an area of consciousness not to be tampered with, unless one is under the guidance of a competent master. The only guides whom I know to be capable of handling persons who get into this field of consciousness are the ECK Masters.

This is the reason why so many neophytes are suddenly plagued with problems, and do not know what is troubling them. They think it comes from some outside cause and put the pressure on to read more, to study deeper works, only to find their troubles increasing. Even the saints can have many of their deep-seated problems laid to this sort of thing, for this is the danger awaiting those who are crying and seeking God too deeply. I discourage this type of thing because too often it leads only to harm for the individual.

One must be prepared physically, mentally, and spiritually

to receive the spiritual forces as they enter into him. Man cannot meet this ECK power without some foundation, without some structure of understanding and knowledge of what It is and how It works. He must develop stamina in the emotional body, and a vitality that will allow him to keep his balance while undergoing certain degrees of intake of this powerful force emitting from the true Godhead.

Inflow of the ECK is affected by the emotional state of mental processes. This is the part of us that becomes aberrated and must be cleared before the full impact of this God power can be of any great benefit to us. This is why I have emphasized the various means of leaving the physical, or human, state of consciousness, and performing in the higher states.

For some reason we have many different types of manners given by the mentalists, metaphysicians and psychotherapists. These are long, drawn out, and given to discussion and argument. We know that on the whole they are a failure, for few seldom get beyond the basic states or attitudes with which the person under therapy entered this world, and what we call his karmic debt from past lives.

In ECK the cause for failure among so many of Its followers is due to five modes of destructive mental action called the five passions. These are perversions of normal faculties that affect the emotional states of the person following ECK. The basic passions are: lust, anger, greed, attachment, and vanity. Any one of these will hold an individual in the physical plane, and keep him from traveling in the worlds beyond.

These passions will dry up the wellsprings of creativity within us. They will bring unthought of aberrations, rising largely from fear and anger. It is fear that concerns us most here, for fear of the unknown is one of the outstanding causes for failure in ECK. To it can be attributed the downfall of many who want to move out of their physical state of consciousness into the higher states.

Fear of the unknown breaks the spirit of the aspirants even before they try any ECK techniques. They are victims of their own emotional imaginings of things lying beyond their physical senses, even beyond their preconceptions of life in the invisible worlds.

Anyone who has this unconscious fear of the unknown—or fear of ridicule from the orthodox—will have a very hard time succeeding at Soul Travel. It is a trap laid by the negative force to keep the aspirant from getting out of the body. It is a greater trap than that offered by anger or vanity, which are themselves formidable factors in keeping people from Soul Travel.

Three creative techniques are presented below. They are actually connected with the ECK, or the Sound Current. This is the creative spirit of God, known to Christians as the Holy Ghost, or Comforter. Metaphysicians call It the Cosmic Power.

We are dealing now with Sound and Light. Therefore, accompanying the spiritual exercises is the Zikar, which is the repetition of the holy names. In the works of ECK we do not dwell upon the state of meditation, as do the Eastern religions.

The first of these three creative techniques is called the Surat technique. Its practice comprises the hearing of Soul, or the melody of ECK. As Soul goes higher and we advance into the inner worlds the music of the ECK becomes greater, until it ultimately merges into the SUGMAD, the Godhead.

The Surat way is rather simple. It is chiefly a spiritual exercise that involves sitting in silence in a fixed position. The participant sits in a straight chair, pulling both feet up under himself in tailor fashion. Putting both hands in his lap, fingers interlaced with palms up, the practitioner places his attention on the Tisra Til, the spiritual eye.

The subject then takes five deep breaths and begins repeating the word HU, the universal name of God. After a considerable length of time has elapsed he takes five more breaths, and continues chanting softly the word HU. It is pronounced as H-U, in a long drawn out manner. His attention remains fixed on the Tisra Til. He does not try to see anything, he just holds it there.

After another considerable lapse of time, he again repeats

his five breaths, bringing them to a total count of fifteen. Following this he slows down chanting the name of God until it is very, very slow. He begins to listen to what he is singing. He gets still slower on the chanting, until vocally it is halted completely. His attention is then switched to listening to the esoteric sounds as the word HU rolls through him. It starts vibrating like a machine and he shakes considerably, but he does not let this frighten him.

Very soon he begins to hear a humming sound in the back of his head, spreading out into his body, until he becomes a part of the sound. Then various parts of the ECK melody start. Sometimes it is the roaring of a waterfall, other times the sounds of violins and/or flutes. This means he is out somewhere on the far planes of the higher worlds, beyond the fifth or Soul plane, and traveling in the Atma body in the realms of God.

These sounds will gradually become a melody of celestial music unlike anything ever heard. Its beauty is so entrancing that he, now in this state of glory and beauty, will actually be in a high state of spiritual consciousness. He falls in love with this godly voice and never wants to return to his earthly role. He has to, though, for it is demanded of him that he serve out his life here before passing on permanently into the worlds of glory.

Only by visiting these heavenly heights and hearing the celestial music does one know that life is nothing within the lower planes. But the danger here lies in his wanting to make his life completely livable in the higher worlds, while still living in the physical body. We do have our duties to perform in this physical world, and we have responsibilities to our families.

In seeking God, too many have found this spiritual enlightenment to be also somewhat of a trap. The glories of it make one shirk his worldly responsibilities. This is the test of Soul, for if we are able to tread the path of ECK and dwell in Its glories we should be practical in our life here on Earth. We should accept what is here, and not allow ourselves to be carried overboard and live a one-sided life.

73

The physical and spiritual must go hand in hand if we are to truly live the life God intends for us. Too much emphasis is placed on God-Realization, with the result that, in some cases, a saint is scarcely more than a spiritual n'er-do-well. Throughout religious history many who made claims to God-Realization—and who actually achieved it—turned out to be of little assistance to their fellow men.

A true follower of God, one who has received the higher realization and dwells in Its state, is generally a hard worker in the physical body. He drives it unrelentingly, until it screams in its fatigue and begs to rest; but the surge of the ECK within him will not let go. It will force him onward in the work of God, pressing him to pass on the message to that plane or world upon which he lives.

He does this quietly, and without the bombastic manner so typical of the missionaries and crusaders of various orthodox faiths. It is done regardless of where the individual may be, whether he is traveling through the worlds beyond this physical one, or while engaged here in his daily routine.

The second of the three creative techniques is called the Nirat. The Nirat technique utilizes the seeing power of Soul, which it uses to witness the subtle entities of the higher worlds. Often, the Soul using this technique will find the path to the other worlds illuminated by Soul's own light, much like the headlights of a car, cutting through the darkness of night, illuminate the road ahead.

As with the Surat technique, the subject sits in silence in a fixed manner. He positions himself in a straight chair, fingers interlaced in the lap, both palms up. He again fixes his attention on the spiritual eye.

This time, however, he puts his mind on the Light, concentrating only on the white Light within the door of the spiritual eye. This is the subtle gateway to the astral world, the first one to pass through on the way to higher worlds.

With his attention fixed on this door, the subject is not to look directly at what has been established on the screen of his mind, but he is to look obliquely. If he stares at it in direct confrontation it will disappear, but once he sees it from a right or left angle on either side of his view, the image of the light stays.

Now very softly he begins to chant the Zikar, the repetition of the holy names of God. If the chela is an initiate, it will suffice to chant his secret word. If not, he chants the names of the various sounds on each plane that he must pass through in order to reach the Soul region. These are: Sola, (physical), Kala, (astral), Aum (causal), Mana (mental), Baju (etheric or unconscious), and SUGMAD (Soul plane).

These are the various Sounds of the ECK as It passes through each plane. By chanting these Sounds the chela is able to lift himself up through the corresponding planes into the Soul world. He begins to see the Light, via the Sound. It is doubtful, though, that he will hear any of the Sounds at this time, for the focus of his attention is on the Light.

This Light of God appears on all planes, but the Light that should interest the chela the most is the Blue Star. It will come into focus after the technique has been practiced for a certain length of time. This star represents the ECK Master, who will appear later in his own radiant body. At the outset the neophyte is not developed enough to witness the living ECK Master inside himself.

Thus the Master appears often as the Blue Star, and sometimes as a misty, pale blue light. The Star or the Light will lead the chela gently onward through the various planes into the Soul region. He must trust it completely, never being doubtful or hesitant about following it, nor wondering where it may lead him.

The Star or globe of Light, as it also appears, should be greeted with rejoicing. The chela should be glad that he has been chosen to witness it. Later, the Light will change on some of the higher planes, into a magnificent white glow. This is the Light of God.

As Soul gets collected and concentrates on the spiritual eye, and before the position is fixed, the chela will have some preliminary experiences of the inner sounds and sights. These occur before Soul is settled down and actually traveling in the inner worlds. Preceding flight he may hear sounds similar to a running train, whistles, and music best characterized as coming from a string instrument of the Western world. Then he will hear sounds like the tinkling of small bells, progressing to the ringing notes of a large bell. Following this are lights similar to the glowing of charcoal, then lightning, and finally the giganticStar appears.

Then he is able to see a whole starry sky. He sees the lightning and moon worlds, and is ready for the ascent. Often, he will see forms as mist, smoke, suns, fire, winds, fire flies lightning, crystals and moons. His attention may be scattered at this point, but it will come back and focus again at a single point.

The third creative technique is like a triad. In it is practiced the Sound, the Sight, and the contemplation of the living ECK Master. He awaits us constantly, each and every one of his chelas, at the threshold of the astral plane, just beyond the sun, moon and lightning worlds. Once he is found the measure of success in Soul Travel can be said to be dependent upon the degree of interest taken in each chela.

This interest lies mainly in the spiritual unfoldment of the disciple, however, and his own interest in Soul Travel, for the purpose of reaching God. If his motive is anything else it is doubtful he will get very far with it. This is another main reason why so many persons do not have success in the works of ECK. Some want it for psychic reasons, others for personal gain; anything but to return to God.

This technique is called the Dhyana, or Tassawar. It is done by gazing steadily at the shining face of the ECK Master on the inner screen of the mind. The chela's attention should be fixed there for at least one-half hour. No longer than this, though, unless he is getting results from his efforts. These results should be that the Master steps into the area of the chela's attention and begins to lift him out of the body to start traveling into the higher worlds.

When he has his attention fixed in this position, the chela starts singing the Master's spiritual name. If it is two names like a first and a last one, then he can use the first one by adding "Ji" to the end of it. The word is pronounced like "gee" and is a title of spiritual respect. It is somewhat similar to "Sir," the title of honor in England.

It is in this position that the Master in his radiant body awaits the chela. He is always here looking for his own beloved follower to arrive in Soul form, either at the time of the physical death of the body, or during the chela's lifetime by means of the spiritual exercises of ECK.

The Master is the leader of the flock, guiding those who will follow him out of the physical state of consciousness and into the realms of the other worlds. First, he takes the chela into the astral world, then the causal, then the mental, and eventually he gets him as far as the Soul plane. Thereafter, they travel together in the true spiritual worlds.

This is the connection in the chela of Soul with the ECK stream of life. It is a liberation, a freedom from the worldy, human state of consciousness. This generally comes when the chela is initiated into ECK for the first time, usually when he takes the Soul Travel Discourses. It is then that he is taken out of the body during sleep, and given the initiation. This is the first; the second is given during full consciousness.

It is in the latter initiation that the chela gets his secret word, and is able to be more fully conscious of traveling in the inner worlds with the living ECK Master.

The living ECK Master is the leader and must be emphatic, concise, and to the point. Never for one moment will he look back to see if his chelas are following nor to count them. He forges ahead, and those who follow must keep on the path of ECK as closely as possible behind him.

The ECK Master never looks back because it is entirely up to the chela to decide whether or not he will follow the Master into the planes of God. This is a personal affair between the Master and the chela, just as it is a personal thing between God and man, for man to want to love and communicate with God. This is his own private and personal interest, and no other man — other than the living ECK Master — should be concerned with this interest.

However, the most important point to bring out here is

that the aspirant must give up his seeking of God. This is the first principle of ECK. It is a strange paradox, especially when compared with the traditional ideal that the only way to the Supreme Being is by an intense desire of the heart. Nothing could be further from the truth than this conception laid down by the early practitioners of mystic consciousness.

Every neophyte must change his goal from seeking to exploit Him to discharging his duty to the Supreme Being in his daily affairs. The sooner the chela learns that his duty and responsibility to God lie in the mastership of his daily affairs, the quicker he gets straightened out to embark on the direct passage into the realm of God. This realization brings the chela immediately to God enlightenment, without making him wait through long, tedious years of work and no results. It also removes the frustration and scattering of attention that plagued him during his earlier attempts to travel the path to God.

Approximately 600 A.D., Sen Ts'an, third patriarch in the famous Chan school of Buddhism, wrote the poem, "Trust in the Heart." It was on this perplexing question: shall we search for God, or just give up and accept what we have? According to this great Chinese student of esoteric wisdom, through trust in the heart, which is our word for consciousness, we can leave behind in a flash the obstructing alternatives of logical reason, and can attain the transcendental realization that is our true goal. This does not separate us from the world of the senses. It only and simply accepts the physical world in its true light, reality and meaning.

As Rebazar Tarzs has always said, the perfect way is difficult, for those who pick and choose. We should neither like nor dislike and all will become clear. Naturally, since there is only a hairbreadth of a difference between transcendental realization and the physical senses, we must cross the line in a non-attached, conscious state. As long as we remain in the state of being either for or against, our progress towards the supreme consciousness is delayed. This struggle, as Krishna told Arjuna in the Bhagavad-Gita, makes man himself a battlefield. In other words, if we accept serenity in God, all obstacles will vanish of their own accord.

Therefore, according to Rebazar Tarzs, we must stop talking, stop thinking, and there is nothing that we cannot understand. If we pursue spiritual illumination, he teaches, it will fade away. If we separate ourselves from God as the doer, we become the searcher, always haunted and always trying to find the Ultimate Reality. So we never seek It, for all we want is here, now. We just need to transcend the body to get the objective view and know all things. Life is keeping in balance.

By doing the spiritual exercises as given in this chapter, one finds that the SUGMAD, the Invisible, may speak at any moment. It might be a message, just a deep breath, a feeling of warmth, or it might be a feeling as though some weight has fallen from your shoulders. But in some way, within a minute or two, you will receive an inner reassurance. "It is done. God is on the field." The chela's work for this period is then completed. He stands consciously in the presence of God, a beholder, watching God at work. It is the insight that counts, for the Voice of God has been manifested; the presence of God appeared and peace was restored in some disoriented place.

This is why the ECK cannot be grasped by human or psychic consciousness. It is the flow of the spiritual power that must be realized. It can be recognized only within ourselves, for we can neither grasp It nor hold It like a thought. It just IS!

All religions and philosophies make reference to their founder or dominating force. This is usually embodied in a personality that once lived in this world. We can take as examples leaders of some of the major religions today. These are Jesus Christ, Buddha, Mahavira, Zoroaster and Mohammed, who are the reference points millions of people today use for spiritual guidance in their lives. But these leaders have gone out of the body now, and their guiding spirits have passed into the higher planes.

Although their words handed down to us are reportedly

still in their original form it is doubtful that they are, for men over the centuries have tampered with them and changed them to suit their own purposes. Also, we are looking to the dead works of departed teachers instead of to the living works of a present Master.

No matter how inspiring a book or the written word may be it is not a guru, and should not be taken as such. Unless the spiritual teacher who is responsible for the written works is living, his writings are only reference points. Neither is the same teacher, or master, of much use to his followers unless he is in the flesh and can act as both the outer and the inner Master.

If living, he is a manifestation of the spiritual power. He is the Word made flesh, and can function in both the outer and the inner worlds. Outwardly he is limited by his own embodiment of flesh, but inwardly he is free to do anything or be anywhere, even in many places at the same time. This is the living ECK Master.

The teachings of the Ascended Masters are of little use to anyone because they are inner teachers only, and without physical embodiment. In other words, they cannot act as channels for the ECK power because they have no vehicle through which to channel It. Therefore it is imperative for any sacred teachings to have a living Master. If they do not, the seeker for truth is wasting his time.

The chela in the human body must have a Master in the human body. This is a fixed law of the ECK. Every Master, when his duties are finished, will hand over his work to another Master who is in the body, who will in turn carry on until he finishes here. All ECK Masters, like Rebazar Tarzs, Fubbi Quantz and Yaubl Sacabi, may live on for years in their physical bodies, far exceeding the normal lifetime of man. Then they will retire and give up their duties to another. However, they still stand in the background, watching and helping the world unfold spiritually toward its higher destination.

One can neither sell nor betray the living Master, for he is a channel of the holy ECK. The slightest act against him returns swiftly to the doer. When one gossips or uses malicious talk about any God-realized being he gets the results in quick doses that are not often pleasant. It is an old cliche that a person prays to get something from the divine Source but is quick to criticize Its channel. This is being two-faced. It is an attempt at deceit and certainly will not work with the spiritual forces, for it is a punishable deed.

This is the real negative trap and no one should ever knowingly fall for its luring whispers. A great many do, but it is easy to work one's way out of such entanglements by straightening out the conditions of the mental argument going on inside the individual. Many simply do not know or understand the nature of the living ECK Master and will take it upon themselves to be snide with him.

They likewise do not understand the troubles that befall them as a consequence of their overt and covert attempts to belittle or ridicule the teachings of the blessed ECK. For some reason, they believe that they are above such things simply because they have read a few books or studied under certain teachers and pseudo-masters. Even the most simple lies will bring about a quick result which is not of a pleasant nature.

One does not realize what these small acts might be, but on closer scrutiny we find that they are such minor things as belittling the Master's words; arguing with him over some point; the posing of needless questions; smoking in his presence; being doubtful of any promise that he makes, whether it be of what is to come into a person's life or some point on ECK; turning against him and refusing to act in accordance with his desires, which are for the benefit of the chela and towards his spiritual unfoldment; and acting snide with the Master. These are some of the things that create a negative attitude towards the living Master.

Of course this is egotism, for the negative power wants the chela in its grasp and will promise anything to keep him there. But the major thing that the Kal never reveals to the chela is that when he creates any overt or covert act against the channel of God, he is creating a heavy karmic debt. He is set back in his progress on the spiritual path of God, and must overcome this burden by starting out again to resolve it. The Master knows and understands this but he never says anything, only watches and waits to give help wherever he is able to do so. The chela is on his own, and whatever he does he must take as self-responsibility.

This is all part of the creativity of ECK, and in the end one finds such negativity to affect him most during the spiritual exercises. He cannot do his best if he is creating even more karma. His efforts at the creative techniques will fall apart and bring him almost nothing by way of results.

Too many people cry out that they practiced the techniques laid down in the discourses and never got anywhere. Little do they think that it is the result of something they are doing against themselves or against the living ECK Master. If one searches out the consciousness or the inner self he will soon find those little hidden parts that have been unconsciously exposed to others, to the outer world, and especially to the living Master.

The change can be made at any time the chela desires it, but he must remember one part of the great law: resolving karma or undoing negative traits within one's self is not the means to the end, but only a step on the path to God.

CHAPTER SIX

THE UNFINISHED CREATION OF GOD

The spheres of those many worlds about us are beyond the imagination of man. Should we think about counting them they would appear to be beyond the number of stars in the heavenly sky. But with the exception of the physical worlds few, if any, of these planes are finished.

Any ECK chela knows that all possible human situations are ready-made states. Rebazar Tarzs confirmed this when speaking to me on the windy slopes of the Himalayan foothills above Darjeeling, "I am the beginning and the end; there is nothing to come that has not already been made and established in the now of time."

He was only quoting the Shariyat-Ki-Sugmad, in which it says that every aspect, every plot and dream of human history has been worked out. All of these are mere possibilities in the records of each individual, as long as he is not experiencing them. Still, they remain the realities of life that we all can experience.

This is how karma operates with each Soul that inhabits a body on Earth. It must experience whatever is possible within that one embodiment, then pass on to another, and eventually go through whatever human situation is possible for each incarnation. We could never experience all situations within one lifetime, so arrangements were made for Soul to have many incarnations — sometimes millions of them — in order to learn as much as possible about this world. When it is finished with them, it becomes purified.

Yaubl Sacabi, spiritual head of the great sacred city of Agam Des, once remarked that "There is a difference between the identity of the individual Soul and states of reality. These states, or conditions, change, but Soul never changes nor ceases to be."

What he means is that we are concerned with states of

consciousness and not imagination, for imagination is not a state. Soul never changes its identity. It only changes its embodiment in its different forms on different planes, until becoming established once more on the fifth plane.

Therefore, we can say that, within human existence, should we be aware of hate, love, or any other states of consciousness within ourselves, it is a condition or a state because it is divided from imagination. It may be an illusion, but it is nevertheless a state of consciousness in which we are living, and of which we are certainly self-conscious at the time.

This is a matter of utmost importance, for it is self-consciousness of the state that makes it reality. The moment the chela realizes this truth — that everything in his world is a manifestation of activity within himself and that the conditions and circumstances of his life reflect the state of consciousness with which he is fused — then everything becomes perfect in accordance with that state.

Experience of this condition makes the chela realize that he is the supreme master of his own world and that the state he identifies himself with will be his subsequent experience in life. He must therefore realize that whatever is his inner state will be his outer physical karma. Until he learns to be free of any belief in a secondary cause, or that he is the effect of anything other than his own state of consciousness, he will always be a victim of the effects of the other or outer, worlds.

The great truth to be remembered here is that we are living in a world of creation that is finished as long as we are within the lower worlds. Our problem is that we work only on parts of it, and never the whole. The spiritual worlds, those above the Soul plane, are the unfinished creations. These are the worlds in which we should dwell, for they are composed of pure spirit and always must conform to whatever Soul desires of it, provided, of course, that Soul is developed enough spiritually to be in a position to take charge. Otherwise, Soul is always led by this unformed essence we know as the ECK.

The whole idea of the ECK is to help clear the individual of his human and spiritual aberrations in a more normal manner than any of the so-called sciences of the mind today. This is proven possible, for the Master will teach the chela how to get himself beyond the worlds of aberrations. This is done by Soul Travel, movement beyond consciousness of human activity.

Too many people think in terms of major processes to get rid of their aberrations. They spend too much money trying to get something done for themselves; trying to make changes within themselves when it is not at all possible. *The secret of change is not within ourselves because it is the world around us that is ever-changing.* We, Souls, are not. All things in the lower planes are states of consciousness, subject to change. We must recognize this. Every human situation is an already-made state, crystallized, set, but too many metaphysicians, preachers and religious leaders are telling us that we must make the changes within to fit the pattern of conformity.

This is altogether the wrong approach. We make no changes in ourselves, but in our false conception of this life principle, that no one can make changes inwardly. We must accept the fact that all events have already been established in this universe and we can only experience them. Trying to make changes in ourselves results in failure that leads to self-guilt, and more often, neurosis.

The chela does not understand that it is not he who makes the changes. He must learn instead to regard these already made states of consciousness from a different, objective viewpoint. Then he can see every aspect, every plot, drama and situation as already worked out, and mere possibilities as long as he is not in them. But once he enters into these situations they constantly present themselves as overpowering realities.

Love, being, and anger, can all become states. Therefore, the chela's position in any world can also become a state. This means that if he has grasped the knowledge of how to change the states within himself and not himself, and can live in the condition of self-consciousness within that state, then he has conquered it. He can live on the astral plane, the causal, mental, etheric and Soul plane, and even in the higher worlds without changing the conditions of his physical

85

self on the physical plane. When the chela lives within he can make changes by changing his state of consciousness.

This has much to do with the chela's character traits, karma, and recognition of what is within himself, in relation to these states of consciousness. The chela must recognize what it is that gives him the ability to move through these states. It is not projection, it is Soul Travel; movement from one state of consciousness to another.

We must remember that imagination is not a state within itself, but only a mental faculty that God has granted us, that we may enter into the first door of the inner worlds. Other than that it is of little use to anyone. Human existence itself is a state, and when the reality of itself becomes a state it is divided from the imagination, and lives within a certain consciousness.

This is a truth known to all, but the trick of it is the self-consciousness of the state. This is living within the state and being aware of all that goes on within it. It is the private universe of the man, which we all have. Each of us carries his own universe with him and this is the world he must have control of and be able to keep for himself. It is his individual privacy.

Once the chela discovers these things he becomes the master of his own universe, which is the microcosm of the whole. It is the state of consciousness with which he is identified that determines his experience. Once he realizes this he is released from what he believed was the original cause but was actually only a secondary cause; that he was the effect of some control from the outer world. Now he is no longer the effect of anything but the cause itself, and he is master of his own destiny.

Thus as long as we are living in the human state of consciousness the world of creation is finished and its original is within ourselves. At the present, then, we are working only in the field of the completed world, for it is on this plane that the original can be found within us. The world of mental activity is manifested before observers' eyes, revealing also the course of time as it jumps the attention between the rest points of eternity. An infinite abyss separates any two moments and we, by the movement of attention, give life to the circumstances within the inner worlds that manifest outwardly.

We must think of the spiritual worlds as containing an infinite number of states of consciousness from which they can be viewed. Think of these states as rooms or mansions in the great spiritual universe, the house of God. And, like the rooms of any house, they are fixed relative to one another. We ourselves are the reality here, Soul, the living but moving occupant of this great spiritual universe. And, on this universe, situations are worked out but they are not in effect until Soul activates them.

Each situation represents certain mental and emotional activities on the lower planes. To enter into any of these planes, or rooms, we must be in agreement with the ideas and feelings represented therein. Each plane has an infinite number of possible mental and emotional transformations that Soul can experience. If it is the astral plane then we will meet with many whom we knew during our lives on earth. This plane has a definite set of rules and beliefs, and in order to change to another state, such as the causal, we must simply adjust ourselves to a change of rules, beliefs and knowledge. Matching the authenticity of the causal state with our own is the way we move to it from the astral. The moment one does this he has travelled from one point in the invisible worlds to another.

Therefore, it is important for any chela on the path of ECK to choose the God-Realized state. This is the highest he can serve. And, once he has chosen it, all other states of consciousness will become lifeless and drop away. This state can be established only one way. As Yaubl Sacabi says, "To live in the pure state one must be and act in purity." All things are made and manifested by the Word made flesh. It is the Sound and the Light that bring into being the pure state.

The ECK chela is thus the "Light of the World," the vehicle by which the ideals he has consented to are made manifest to all within his sphere. He lives at the core of this enlightened state and truth radiates from this center. He never thinks from it but lives and manifests from this, the heart of all. It is only from the state of God-Consciousness that what one thinks and acts is ever manifested in the outer worlds.

The chela becomes absorbed with the ideal state he wants to realize. He must have a definite set of goals or the mind will wander, and in its wandering take in every negative suggestion it hears. Nothing is more important than the goals on which the mind feeds. If we feed on those thoughts springing from our ideals then life becomes one with the state of God-Consciousness. We are not seeking God but find that we are living within His splendor.

The chela must therefore assume the feeling of already being in the state of God-awareness. He does not do this for a few moments only, but accepts it as part of his own self and carries it around like the fragance of a rose. It establishes itself in the magnetic field around him and influences all that come within its orbit. Once it gains a foothold it is very hard to dispel. The crucial point, however, is *living* within the core of the God State and never *hoping* that you might.

To do this one applies the concept of polarity. Polarity simply means the state of opposition between two related factors: light and darkness, heat and cold, material and unsubstantial, harmony and discord, positive and negative, good and evil, male and female. Nothing in this world can exist except in relation to its opposite poles.

On this plane we have to work with the polarity of light and darkness. This is one of the most interesting aspects of spiritual Light. While we are still working in the lower worlds we will not be raised to the highest; not until everything is Light and no shadows are found. This is something we must think of when beginning the path to God.

It is only natural that in the physical life we think constantly in terms of light and shadow, but this is only a part of the lower worlds. We cannot work in this field without realizing that we gain experience in the physical universe by living in both the shadows and the light. We must learn to live within both opposites, and unless we are well drilled in this lesson our advancement is delayed on the spiritual path.

Only when persons approach the great Masters to ask them personal favors, to know something about their own problems, do we begin to get an insight into the human condition. Then we learn that the lower part of self cannot be satisfied and there is little need to try to fulfill any of its desires.

It is this outer nature of man that we always encounter when trying to introduce him to the spiritual works of ECK. It balks, fights any changes, and will not allow itself to be put in any position that makes it differ from the conformity of all human nature. It never allows any interference with its own belief, and as it is made of the negative materials in life, it will battle anything of a spiritual nature that tries to enter its realm.

The basic fight it puts up is doubt and skepticism. It will not accept any evidence because the negative, or just plain human nature, will never allow the positive any foothold. Unbeknownst to it, though, most of the great saints and believers in God started right within this realm, expressing the greatest amount of skepticism. The ECK enters this mass of doubt in small amounts at first, then gradually bores its way into the opposition and eventually wins.

A basic principle in ECK is that at one time or another all bodies within the physical atmosphere must come to rest. Soul Travel is based on this whole principle. If Soul inhabits a body in this world, it must learn to leave it daily and dwell in the upper worlds, which is its true home. Someday the body must come to rest, or die, as it is known on this plane, so Soul trains the body to fend for itself. It then lives as much as possible in the heavenly worlds. These must become part of our own world. Then the living Self will dwell with God while the human part lives on Earth, as expressed in the old axiom: "My heart is in Heaven while my feet are on Earth."

We are a part of all things, yet as individuals in Soul bodies we are accountable only to God. Someday the body will come to rest, and Soul must be prepared not to let itself be trapped in some other body in this physical environment, nor in some astral shell that has no control over itself.

The difference between the finished and the unfinished creations is that God, the SUGMAD, established the lower, finished worlds, for the purpose of providing a training ground for Soul. After its creation in the heavenly realm Soul is sent to earth as an untried, inexperienced entity. On earth it is like a child who must complete his scholastic work before going out into life and being fitted into society.

Eventually, after many incarnations, Soul is purified by its experiences and returns to heaven. There it is ready to serve God as a co-worker in some spiritual mission. Soul has by then gained experience in the spiritual sense and can choose what it wishes to do in either the spiritual or spirito-materialistic worlds. It may become a planetary spirit, an angel, a cherub, an agent of God, or it may take any spiritual position as a co-worker with God as desired.

Little does one realize that everytime we acquire a new body on earth in our successive line of different incarnations only Soul itself retains any knowledge of other lives already lived. God seems to draw a curtain down on our knowledge of past lives and only lets us remember what has taken place in the particular one we are living.

It is only when we start looking to Soul patterns that all begins to clear up about our past lives. Once this happens we soon learn who we are and what our great mission in this life is. Then we start working to get back into the heavenly worlds. No one can tell us about this. It must be our own experiences that make it possible. Unless an ECK Master brings us to this level of spiritual understanding, then we are without any possible opportunity of returning to the heavenly worlds.

This brings us to the point of the four levels of spiritual petition to God. These are not the usual types of common prayer with the religious fervor of the saints or that known to readers of occult works. It is reaching into the depths of the spiritual powers to remove those blocks standing between Soul and God.

90

These four levels are very simple. They are, first: petition, or Asha. This is the lowest method for trying to get a spiritual or materialistic request fulfilled. Many use this type of request, for its simplicity is designed for those who have no other means of asking God for something. It is to beg, seek, or ask of the Divine Deity something that is beyond the seeker's own realm of getting. Christ's statements in the Gospels, "Seek and ye shall find," or "Knock, and the door shall be opened," are an aspect of orthodox teachings, but this has been over used and abused until the general attitude toward it has become somewhat jaded. We cannot go on forever trying to petition God when there is no answer. This is what causes so many people to give up and never even try.

What we all must remember here is that in order to gain something from the invisible worlds we must be at a certain level of life. If we are below that level of receiving then it never shall be ours. What we do receive is in exacting amount to the spiritual development we have gained. If we get nothing it is very possible that we have not made any progress spiritually. These are points to remember.

Rebazar Tarzs said that in order to receive anything from God we must be open to acceptance. Too many persons are not independent enough to accept anything from anyone. Too many are dependent upon one another, and this is not a point for anyone to forget. The petitioner must get inside himself to see if life is worthy of his demands, for it never serves anyone who begs and pleads for anything.

The second level of spiritual petition is prayer, or Bhakti. So much has been written about prayer and what it can do with and for anyone that it is almost pointless to say anything further. It is, however, the most overrated form of reaching God that anyone could attempt. The religious bodies have made prayer such a mysterious, secret sort of gathering up something for oneself that it has become a much abused manner of approaching God.

For the millions who use this form of approach it can scarcely be said to work. The problem is that it is difficult

91

to know how far religious theories and methods of prayer can be made available to the untrained person. Such an individual is apt to get hold of things by the wrong end and so enmesh himself that he comes up with totally unexpected problems. This is the praise or thankfulness part of the overall approach into the heart of God.

The Lord's Prayer is supposedly the model of all prayers, designed for those with no other means of raising their vibrations. It is judged that Christ, however, had no intention of giving prayers of this nature to any who followed him, but the Gospel writers in the centuries following his death made more out of his words than were actually ascribed to him during his ministry on Earth.

Bhakti is the devotional stage of requesting something from God. Both prayer, Bhakti, and Asha, petition, are still in the karmic realm. The petitioner must therefore accept whatever he gets along with the success of his request. I knew a woman who wanted to get rid of her husband and marry again, but the man she was supposedly in love with had little money. In order to have enough for herself and her children, should she remarry, it meant that her husband would have to leave this life by accident. Then she could get a double indemnity. Her mental prayers for getting rid of her husband and getting some money were almost successful. Only a change in plans caused him to take a train instead of a plane on one of his business trips. The plane crashed in a freak accident and all on board died. The woman gave up her plans and forgot the pseudo love affair.

The third level of spiritual petition is meditation, or Samadhi. This is only a mental form of worship, in a sense: that is, concentrating upon some goal for endless hours until it is reached. The practitioner of this type of worship sits in silence, his thoughts single-tracked, his senses subdued and his gaze fixed at the point of his nose in an unseeing manner. He also applies the Hindu sacred word AUM, and that is all there is to it. Usually, though, the average person cannot do this sort of spiritual practice because he lacks control over his mind and thoughts.

The very word meditation is misleading to Western religious followers. It is so common today that we compare it with prayer and use it in our daily language, when a century ago few if any would have known what we were speaking about. But it has become a much abused practice because the yogis have put too much emphasis upon it, and never carried it above the mental plane.

The sixth chakra in the psychic body of man is known as the Do-Dal-Kanwal, the two-petalled lotus. It is situated in back of the eyes on a level with the lower part of the eyeballs, but exactly in the center of the brain cavity. It is at a point in the subtle body corresponding to the position of the pineal gland. This is the seat of the mind and Soul, which is also the center of control over the body.

Above this center is another one called the Char-Dal-Kanwal, whose function is to supply the four-fold Antishkarans [mental faculties] of the mind with centers of action. These four faculties are: first, the Manas, the faculty of receiving and tasting. This is the mind stuff itself. Second, Buddhi, the intellect, the instrument of thought, discrimination and decision. Third, Chitta, the faculty that takes note of form and beauty, and fourth, Ahankar, a faculty that executes orders once they are given.

Above this center comes the Tisra Til, the third eye, at which all attention is concentrated when meditating. Soul is said to reside in the Do-Dal-Kanwal, which is the highest center in the Pinda or physical universe, and also in the physical body of man. From this center the meditator concentrates his attention on the Tisra Til center, skipping the Antishkaran center. In this manner the attention crosses the line of the Pinda and enters the Anda, the lowest of the other worlds. This is the astral zone, the capitol of which is known as Sahasra-dal-Kanwal. Soul is then on its way along the upper paths in its journey to God. This is the only place for those who know very little about the art of meditation to launch Soul according to this method.

Generally, the Orientals love to preach that meditation is the panacea for all problems. But sooner or later we come to learn that all they are referring to is the mental realm, which eventually becomes the effects of their own efforts.

We find that this Oriental type of meditation brings little more than visions that must be separated to determine reality from the pseudo. So many of these visions are from within the practitioner's own little universe, but he accepts them as something sent by the Supreme Deity as part of the universal worlds. The practitioner regards them as a reward for his faith and devotion in keeping to his periods of meditation.

This self-deception is not always the individual's fault. He has nothing by which to measure these subjective experiences so he must accept them as truth or falsehood. They are usually taken as truth because the meditator does not know any better. In comparison, the spiritual exercises of ECK give its own participants a yardstick to measure whether the reality gained from out-of-the-body consciousness is truth.

Thus we say that meditation is merely a passive state in which one tries to draw God-Realization into himself while sitting in the Asana position to attain oneness with God. The practitioner hopes the attributes of God will descend into himself within the physical body and act as a panacea for all ills.

The next stage on the path is contemplation, known to ECK chelas as the Anitya. This is to direct attention to some object, to muse upon it and study it, or simply ponder the matter.

Contemplation differs from meditation because the object or vision gives purpose to our attention. It is a natural point of concentration. The practitioner scans his subject with the attitude of knowing, coupled with awareness and judgment. Meditation practically makes it a case of either concentrate or fail, while contemplation does not do this.

Contemplation is getting very close to the highest form of worship, for it carries the practitioner beyond the mental planes and into the fifth or Soul plane. This is because the main starting point is the crown chakra, the Sahasra-dal-

Kanwal, or the thousand-petalled lotus. By contemplating this region one begins to travel via the path of ECK into the higher realms.

We are dealing here with levels of consciousness and not creations of a fertile imagination. Neither are we talking about worlds within, but again about levels of consciousness. As Rebazar Tarzs once said, "These are rooms within the palace and must be considered only in this manner. We are going from the smaller rooms into the larger only through the state of Soul movement, which is moving the attention from one point to another."

The attention is withdrawn from the outer world and placed at the top of the head, then held there in contemplation of whatever the practitioner desires. It must be on the higher truths, though, or failure will occur. Then these levels of consciousness, call them worlds if you must, exist only for us, for the outer worlds have been shut out completely from our consciousness.

Slowly Soul will gather up all its forces at the crown chakra until it finally penetrates the inner aperture, leaving the physical world altogether and entering into a higher region. At this particular moment Soul passes through the inner gates of Light and steps into a new world.

This has nothing to do with the Kundalini, which is one of the so-called mystical forces within man. The Kundalini comes under an entirely different type of training, mainly yoga exercises. It has nothing to do with the spiritual exercises of ECK. Nor have many spiritual travelers who have gained the higher planes found much use for the release of the Kundalini until self-control and mental purity have been established over it.

The next and final step is the Hukikat or Nirvikalpa. This is the deepest form of Samadhi, in which the meditator cannot distinguish himself from the object of meditation. This is part of the highest form of contemplation, but we use the word meditation because it is more familiar to the reader.

All the previous steps in prayer or meditation are only

preparation to the Hukikat stage. This is entering into oneness with Truth and Reality.

But here we must stop and explain something that has always bothered students of the spiritual works. We never "become one with God," as the metaphysicians and religionists claim. What actually happens is that we become one with Spirit, the essence of God. This is what is so often poetically named the Breath of God.

There is no pranayama in ECK. Therefore, tne practitioner is not tied to the lower worlds via breath control. His mind must be detached from this world and put upon the radiant form of the ECK Master who is always with him, no matter where he might be in physical distance. The Zikar comes before the Dhyana with the Master. Then following this comes the Bhajan, a form of exercise not known to any other system. It consists in listening to the ECK, the Sound, the Audible Life Stream.

This abstract Sound has many names, but we know It as the ECK. All space is filled with It and It is the Sound of all revelation to the Masters. It is always going on within, around and about man, but he does not usually hear It because his consciousness is centered entirely in his material universe. When we can hear this heavenly music, though, all other Sounds become indistinct to us.

Now you should be able to understand what is meant when someone in ECK claims that the living ECK Master is the ECK Itself. He has become one with the ECK and It has penetrated him until finally no action, either in the Soul, mental or physical realm, is performed unless it is directed by the ECK. He has become the Channel for God.

How one reaches these spiritual heights cannot be put into words. These heights do exist and a very few do reach them, but they cannot describe just what the results were and what their experiences have been. It is literally impossible to say that an individual can get into these heights by any specific technique. The story of St. Francis' sufferings and his desires to have the experience of God are beyond the conception of the normal senses. So are the stories of any saint who has reached these heights. This is also true of the lives of the ECK Masters, for Sudar Singh, the great ECK Master of Allahabad, India, was the son of a wealthy merchant who gave up everything to get this experience in God. His story is most inspiring to the followers of ECK.

In his youth Sudar Singh, like St. Francis, gave up an inheritance that would have left him well off for the rest of his life without lifting a hand. But wealth meant nothing to Sudar Singh. He gave away his rich clothing and went off in rags to become a beggar, that he might rid himself of a stigma hindering his way to God.

He had to learn that a chela must obey without asking questions. This is the essence of the relationship between the Master and chela. But first he had to find a Master, and this was the most important part of his seeking. He announced this to many of his friends and bravely went out to find his Master. But pride and vanity were standing in his way because he believed that giving up his wealth was all that was needed to become established on the path to God.

Like all others Sudar Singh had much to learn. He went to the home of a very important government official who invited him there to study ECKANKAR, but Sudar Singh was somewhat bored at this idea. Meanwhile, Rebazar Tarzs appeared to this government official in his home and told him that Sudar Singh was coming to visit for a few days to ask questions about his Master. Since he was the living ECK Master that this young man was seeking, he would like to be there acting in the role of a servant to wait upon him.

Sudar Singh arrived a few days later, very proud of his rags, and spent approximately thirty-six hours there asking question upon question. Meanwhile, the pseudo servant whose duty it was to wait on the young seeker, patiently stood around in his disguise to see what course of action he would follow.

Several days later Sudar Singh left, very disappointed that he had not fulfilled his quest in his host's home. He completely overlooked Rebazar Tarzs and on leaving remarked, "There is nothing in ECKANKAR for me."

He went from city to city asking questions and hoping to get the answers. His search lasted a year before truth dawned on him. He was in the foothills of the Himalayan mountains north of Darjeeling, when one hot afternoon he stopped to rest. Hungry and tired, he began to wonder if this was the end of all, and if he should return to his father's home and ask forgiveness. He fell into a light sleep.

Suddenly he was awakened by a sound. There was a man with shining, coal black eyes, short dark hair and a beard standing beside him with a pitcher of milk. "I am Rebazar Tarzs," the man said, "he whom you have been searching for. Meet me in the old market place of Srinagar one month from today, and I will accept you as my chela to learn the secrets of heaven."

We are not all this fortunate, but the road is always open for anyone who wants to work his way through the successive levels to dwelling in constant bliss. It is then that we find there is a vastness, a depth and a broadness about ECK that most of us fail to grasp. Unless we find this and understand it, and unless we compare it with history and the other aspects of human existence, then we should stop, for we shall not go any further.

It also means that anytime anyone begins the way of ECK he should stop searching through books and other means of reaching God. We cannot travel two paths at the same time. This does not mean that we should become dogmatic about ECK, but the troubles we encounter on Its path are due mainly to the fact that we cannot give up preconceived notions and ideas about our spiritual destiny, and all that goes with it.

Therefore, whoever is capable of lifting himself into the areas beyond the Soul plane will open himself as a channel for God. This is one of the most important features of ECKANKAR, if it is not already known. It means that all who want to serve God and become a co-worker with Him must sooner or later step across the dividing line between the spirito-materialistic worlds and the spiritual worlds.

When one begins his ascent to heaven he first becomes the

chela, which is followed by being an initiate, then an Acolyte, then the Mahdis, and finally the Adept. These are the stages that he will go through, until he finally enters into the Ancient Order of the Vairagis to become a Master.

His turn will come to be the living ECK Master, should it be so established among the hierarchy of the Vairagis Order. If not, there are other duties that he may take up and perform in the spiritual development of those trying to find their way back to heaven again.

Chapter Seven

THE STEPS TO THE SECRET KINGDOM

The factors that are to be discussed in this chapter concern knowing, faith, realization, and experience. All of these are steps into the secret kingdom of God. Without any of these parts we are apt to slip on the path and have a hard time recovering.

Here the chela must consider something that is the foundation of work in ECK. As Rebazar Tarzs once said: "It takes actual experience for the chela before belief can enter into him." This is a fact that the majority of seekers of God overlook, for without experience none can have realization.

This is the most important factor of life in the spiritual worlds, for without experience we do not have either knowing, faith, or realization. We must remember that each is a step to the state we know as experience in God, for they fit together as a glove fits the fingers.

During a Southern tour of the United States some time ago someone at the Fort Lauderdale workshop asked, "Can you prove all this about God worlds and realization?" I answered in the negative and left the question hanging for the benefit of the person who had asked it. I cannot prove individual experience and this is exactly why science does not accept the God-Realized state. None can know it except he who has experienced it.

My contention is that anyone who has never reached the God-Realized state is apt to believe in something false. It is a state of the unknown until he experiences it. He is in the position of the man who has read everything about how to play golf, but until he gets out on the green and swings a club, it is still in the theoretical stage. He is dealing with belief, or the realm of fantasy, the area in which so many seekers of God fall when trying to travel the path alone. They often become neurotics, paranoids, and perhaps even schizophrenics. This is the danger of trying to read too much in the occult field, or in overloading oneself with the various discourses many groups sell.

Experience, properly interpreted and understood, leaves no doubt in the mind of him who has participated in it. Invariably, it is but a piece of semantics for the God-seeker, and he should not be too interested in philosophical belief as his goal. He must know that the experience is true. Until he has experienced Self and God-Realization, he really does not know one thing about it. He can talk and read everything, but he has still in no way contacted the reality of it.

I have said a hundred times in seminars throughout the world that, "I can write a million or two words on the subject of God-Realization, talk for hours on end, write books and tell the world about this glorious phenomenon, but until one experiences it, it means nothing to him." It is but words I say or write, which all come back into the mental realm and mean nothing until the reality of the subject is achieved. Then we know.

This is the difference between knowledge and knowing. Knowledge is only information, and the one with a head full of knowledge is often a failure at everything. This is why so many college graduates cannot perform in our society; knowledge is stuffed into their heads by ivy tower professors who believe that this is the only way to make society work. Few professors have the experience necessary in life to make the student a greater member of the society he has to live in for the rest of his mortal days.

The chela often reaches the stage wherein faith and belief hold little comfort for him, because he has recognized the reality of God's truth. Yet he has hardly had any realization of the living ECK Master, who is known as the MAHANTA of the age. When someone writes or speaks about his troubles with the spiritual exercises of ECK, it is generally because he is a novice and does not really know what he is getting into when taking up the spiritual path of ECK.

Primarily he gets himself tangled in philosophical jargon

and pseudo logic, and finally ends by drowning in a sea of intellectuality. He really believes that all he has to do is follow the set of exercises laid down in the discourses and success will be his own. But this is not true for he soon finds himself in real trouble. He cannot achieve success with the exercises and this makes him an effect of his own effects, which is about the worst thing that could happen.

The truth of the matter is that the path to God is a lonesome road. The more quickly the chela learns that nobody [except the MAHANTA] will be with him while traveling his highway to heaven, the quicker will he know that success with anything like the spiritual exercises will come only by his own efforts. Nobody can help him. He has to learn to rely on no one but himself. The MAHANTA will always be with him, but he is going to let the chela work out his own problems as much as possible. He never intends to make ECK a spiritual welfare program.

At the present we can give twelve steps into the Secret Kingdom of God. These steps correspond with the various planes and are: the physical, Astral, Causal, Mental, Etheric (upper part of the mental plane), Soul, Alakh, Alaya, Hukikat, Agam, Anami, and the Sugmad, the Ocean of Love and Mercy and the SUGMAD, Living Reality, which is considered the Godhead.

The deeper reason for why we call these the steps is that too many seekers of God feel that it is a rather less strenuous approach to the Godhead than that of other religious groups. One has to take a good look at the road he is to travel before entering upon it, for we have to meet the MAHANTA at the place where the three roads meet and all except Soul are slain. This means that the lower self and the mind must be done away with so that Soul is released from their hold and free to travel the high road.

One must take into consideration all the planes he must meet during his travels to the Godhead. Here we start at the lowest plane:

1. Physical Plane. Its sound is contained in the word

Alayi; the classical name is Elam. This world is described as the Pinda in the Hindu language, and it is the region of the illusion of reality (maya), science, body, day to day events in life. This is the first step on the road to the Secret Kingdom.

2. Astral Plane. Its word is Kala and its classical name is Sat Kanwal-Anda. It is described by the Hindus as Tirkya Pad. It is the source of all psychic phenomena, ghosts, flying saucers, spirits, etc. This is the highest plane reached by astral projection and most occult sciences.

3. Causal Plane. Its word is Aum and its ruler is Maha Kal Brahm. This is the region where the memory patterns of past lives hold sway. It is here that all those who can do Akashic readings for others look for the source of trouble in past lives and re-embodiments. On this plane one can hear the tinkling of bells. It is the plane of negative reality which affects all below.

4. Mental Plane. Its sound is the word Mana. This is where the ruler of the three worlds of Vedanta, Buddhism and Hinduism dwells. He is the Brahm, the Great Brahman spoken of so much in the Hindu sacred writings. It is the source of philosophy, ethics, moral teachings, and the understanding of conventional Gods and religions. In ECK we realize that in reality this is the home of the Kal Niranjan, the God of the lower worlds and ruler of the negative forces. He is known by many names, including Satan, the Devil, Asmodeus, Beelzebub and Ahriman, to name a few. The negative power is often known as the Universal Mind, which many sects and religions worship as the true God power, but this is only part of the illusion used by the Kal to keep its hold as Soul tries to get back to the heavenly worlds again.

Etheric Plane. It is the top of the Mental Plane. Its word is Baju. This is what the psychologists would call the unconscious plane. It is the source of primitive thought, and is a very thin sheath between the mental body and the Atma Sarup, the Soul body. Primitive people were closer to this body than any others because, with the development of civilization, racial and individual aberrations also developed in the other bodies of man. Few people, if any, despite the various books and literature appearing for public reading, know anything about the unconscious mind. Many call it the subconscious, but it is really more unconscious than this because it is a clearer channel for those who are seeking to become instruments of God. The ruler here is one whom we know as the Saguna Brahm; known also as Par Brahm.

Now we come to the dividing line between the lower and the upper worlds. This line separates the psychic regions from the spiritual planes and is known to the chelas as one of the two grand divisions of the universes of God. Always within the lower worlds we encounter the problems of karma and reincarnation. This is the burden every Soul must bear while undergoing his training within the lower worlds. In the upper regions we gain freedom and self-recognized individuality which allows Soul to re-enter into that state called God-consciousness.

5. Soul Plane. This is the first plane that Soul enters in the pure spiritual worlds. The words here is SUGMAD, with each individual letter spelled out, and the Light is more brilliant than the imagination can comprehend. The ruler of this plane is Sat Nam. He is the first manifestation of God before going into the worlds of the second grand division, called Atma Lok.

6. Alakh Lok. Lok means "plane" in the Hindu language. This is the world many mystics who are able to get into the higher regions believe to be the end of all life, the abode of God, the Ultimate Reality. The word of this invisible plane is Shanti, pronounced Shawn-ti. Those who reach this plane must have power of discrimination to go beyond it, for they find such peace and happiness here after establishing themselves in it.

7. Alaya Lok. This is the endless world, called so because it is so huge there seems to be no end to it. It is often called

THE GOD WORLDS

NAME OF PLANE	WORD	CLASSICAL NAME	SOUND
ABOVE 12 PLANES. . . **AKSHAR REALIZATION**			
12. SUGMAD	UNSPOKEN WORD	SUGMAD-LIVING REALITY	MUSIC OF GOD
11. SUGMAD WORLD	UNSPOKEN WORD	SUGMAD LOK	MUSIC OF UNIVERSE
10. ANAMI LOK	HU	ANAMI LOK	SOUND OF A WHIRLPOOL
9. AGAM LOK	HUK	AGAM LOK	MUSIC OF THE WOODWINDS
8. HUKIKAT LOK	ALUK	HUKIKAT LOK	THOUSAND VIOLINS
7. ALAYA LOK	HUM	ALAYA LOK	DEEP HUMMING
6. ALAKH LOK	SHANTI	ALAKH LOK	HEAVY WIND
5. SOUL	SUGMAD	SAT NAM	SINGLE NOTE OF FLUTE
---------- DIVIDING LINE BETWEEN PSYCHIC ----------			
ETHERIC TOP OF MENTAL	BAJU	SAGUNA-SAGUNA BRAHM INTUITION	BUZZING OF BEES
4. MENTAL	MANA	BRAHMANDA BRAHM MIND	RUNNING WATER
3. CAUSAL	AUM	MAHA-KAL-PAR-BRAHM MEMORY	TINKLE OF BELLS
2. ASTRAL	KALA	SAT KANWAL-ANDA EMOTION	ROAR OF THE SEA
1. PHYSICAL	ALAYI	ELAM. . .SENSES	THUNDER

OF ECK. . .

DESCRIPTION

...COVERS ALL WORLDS

OCEAN OF LOVE AND MERCY. . .

Above the SUGMAD are many planes not yet realized...

NAMELESS PLANE - Beyond human language - we can hardly speak of it. . .

INACCESSIBLE PLANE - Few enter into this world - no words can describe it. . .

HIGHEST STATE Soul generally reaches - Soul stays here for eons. . .

ENDLESS WORLD - SACH KHAND - Eternity seems to begin and end here - unknown world. . .

INVISIBLE PLANE - Soul finds peace and happiness - does not want to leave. . .

DIVIDING PLANE - First realm of the SUGMAD - pure spirit - pure being - Self-Realization. . .

------------ AND SPIRITUAL WORLDS ------------------------------------

UNCONSCIOUS - Source of the primitive. . .

JEHOVAH - Source of philosophy - ethics - moral teachings - aesthetics - Universal Mind Power - God of Religions. . .

KAL NIRANJAN - Rules over negative reality - affects all below. . .

TIRKYA PAD - Source of all psychic phenomena - flying saucers - spirits, etc. Highest reached by astral projection and most occult sciences. . .

PINDA - Illusion of reality - maya - science - day to day "life" - plane of matter - energy - space - time - Soul trapped by the five passions - lust - anger - greed - attachment - vanity. . .

the Sach Khand plane, and appears to be the unknown world where eternity begins and ends. Yet it is only another spiritual plane that appears to be mammoth because of its vastness. The word here is Hum—like the sound of humming with the lips closed, a swarm of bees, or a high electrical sound. We hear it in practically everything in our daily existence, but do not recognize it.

8. Hukikat Lok. This is the highest state Soul generally reaches, but it can still go on into worlds beyond it. When Soul arrives on this plane it often has to stay for eons before passing on to the next. The word here is Aluk, pronounced as A-Luk, with a long sounding of the second part of the word.

9. Agam Lok. Followers of ECKANKAR know this as the inaccessible plane, for few, if any, ever enter into it. Here the word is *Huk*, a short barking sound made with the deep part of the throat. This world is so brilliant there are never any words to describe it. The old mystics used to use sign language to describe any journey to these high worlds. The same would apply here.

10. Anami Lok. This is known as the nameless plane, for there is nothing to say about it. It is beyond the vocabulary of any human language. The most to be said about it is the single word representative of the Anami Lok. This word is HU, the universal name of God, which is present in every existing language. It is present in the words we speak, in the sound of animals; it is the wind in the trees, the rushing of waters, the roaring of water falls, the beat of the sea against a beach or stone cliff. It is everywhere, in every plane below it. We can hardly speak of it.

11. SUGMAD World. ECKANKAR does not say there are only twelve planes, for above the Anami Lok there are numerous ones not yet accounted for in the explorations of the ECK Masters. But in order not to confuse ECK chelas we give only the number listed here. Also, one must remember that there are many planes listed within these twelve regions.

12. SUGMAD. This is the SUGMAD, Living Reality, the Ocean of Love and Mercy. Above this is the AKSHAR Realization which covers all worlds. The sound here is the Music of God, and it can only be experienced, never put into words.

Some explorers of the spiritual worlds list fifty or so planes within each world, but this is not quite true, for we know the astral world contains over one hundred different planes. These are not exactly planes but states, similar in geographical nature to the states and provinces within each divided region of the physical. In the higher worlds, above the fifth world, we do not seem to find divisions of this nature. All is one complete world of its own on each plane. Understand that we work with the whole instead of parts upon reaching the true spiritual worlds.

The chela must think in terms of allness in the true spiritual worlds. This part of his awareness apparatus works differently on the various planes he must go through in order to reach the Godhead. Therefore, we are never without some state of awareness, even in the mineral stage of consciousness. This awareness is one-pointed on the lower planes, but upon reaching the true spiritual planes it becomes omnipresent, or multiple. In other words, one can see in all directions when Soul is in the higher worlds.

It is for this very reason that the MAHANTA, who is the living ECK Master, will take the chela through the lower planes first, going gradually into the state of God-Realization instead of immediately. The purpose of this is to keep the chela balanced in his physical life. Too many have been pushed and shoved into the higher state only to return and find themselves no longer fit for life here in this world.

Fanatical religious figures have at times dominated history like Rasputin, who touched the God-consciousness state and then reduced himself to the psychic element, due to the nature of his times. Rasputin, and others like him, abused the God-conscious state to become destroyers instead of builders. They lacked a Master who could have carried them safely through the lower worlds into the spiritual heaven. It is said that today we are confusing psychic experiences for the spiritual state. This happens because no one has a measuring rod by which he can compare the differences between psychic and spiritual experiences.

The faculties within Soul actually correspond with the invisible planes I have given here. The planes are then influenced in turn by these faculties of Soul. It is a give and take affair, and unless we are able to understand what is going on within Soul the individual is apt to become lost and flounder about.

Many persons are ignorant of the existence of the inner planes and these Soul faculties. However, anyone who observes life flowing past in the world around him cannot fail to see the tides in the affairs of people that cannot be explained by the material sequence of cause and effect. Therefore, it is these subtle tides that the ECK Master studies, formulating the laws in regard to them, and guiding the chelas through the rocks and shoals of daily life.

Contrary to widespread belief among those studying various spiritual works, these planes do not lie one above the other. They are simply different modes of existence and can, any and all of them, occupy the same space at the same time just as light, sound and temperature do. The different aspects of consciousness are built up out of these different forms of existence, just as the calcium that forms the bones of the body is taken from the mineral kingdom of earth, and the water found in bodily tissues is drawn from springs and rivers.

This calcium is in no way different from the calcium to be found in plant tissue or the rocks of the earth's surface. The heart is a pump like any pump, and water in the blood is no different in its action than water in hot water pipes. Therefore, the same condition should prevail in the sphere of consciousness. The spark of divine ECK, the innermost core and nucleus of every Soul, is also part of the God realm.

Thus mental power with its force and images is part of the kingdom of mind, the mental plane. Memory and recall of past lives belong to the causal plane; our emotional and instinctive nature is part of the astral world, and the physical body is part of the earth kingdom. It should be remembered, though, that the earth has a subtle electro-magnetic aspect as well as a dense one. This fools people doing psychic research, for they believe that this electro-magnetic part of the physical body is something greater than the earthly part of it.

One thing I should like to interject is the thin layer between the mind and Soul, which is the unconscious part of the mind. Its powers are part of the upper mind region wherein lie the worlds of instinct and the sympathetic nervous system of the body.

The physical body receives impressions from the physical plane through the five physical senses. It cannot perceive thought, emotion, or things of the spirit except as they are signalled to it by the effect they have on the body. There are perceptive senses, very elementary in most people but very highly developed in some, that correspond with the various levels of consciousness given in the above paragraphs.

We are influenced far more than we realize by the unconscious states of those around us. This is the reason why good morale is important in any organization.

This is also true of any state or nation, for any minority group with a sense of outrage or injustice can upset and demoralize a whole nation of people, a government, or a private business. A dictator wins popular support by appealing to the moral injury of minority groups and eventually brings down the established government. Then he replaces the governmental head and rules with an iron hand, failing to see that whatever method he used to bend the minority groups to his purposes will be used by another against him.

Governments believing that they can foster revolutions in other countries and dissolve the established law and order forget—or overlook—the fact that whenever they do this the same happens in their own country. It all boils down to one fact: the inharmonious person works up all kinds of resistances around himself and makes life rough going for himself. History has proven this out. The ways of Alexandra, for example, wife of Nicholas II, added to the downfall of the Czars of Russia in 1918.

These factors are overlooked by the chela whose main interest is focused upon himself. Should he become powerful in his mental forces without the proper discipline, he could bring ruin upon himself and those around him. Rasputin, the mad monk of Russia, is an outstanding example of this. Napoleon is another whose tremendous mental powers and influence caused a major upheaval of Europe and changed the map of the continent.

Rebazar Tarzs said once in a visit, "Nothing should move the dweller in ECK! He must live in God and nothing else. The influence of the psychic worlds shall not touch him."

The chela does not want to get into areas of meditation that carry him only into the psychic regions. So many of the Oriental religions hardly let a person get above these planes. Naive people, posing as religious leaders, often lead their even more naive followers into areas of danger by not being able to give them spiritual assistance in the psychic worlds.

So many people want to alter their environment until they have control over it and can achieve happiness. This is literally impossible, but it has nevertheless bothered the people of the world since the beginning of time. The history of the earth plane is built upon this false precept and countless fiction stories were established because the writer believed it to be the basis of happiness. This is not true, for no individual nor group of people can change the environment to suit themselves without hurting others. It is the same old story that whatever one does to take control of the environment never suits the desires and needs of those around him.

This basic factor is the cause of all social ills within the world. Reformers and churches are preaching peace to those more naive than themselves. We can never have peace on this planet because it is impossible; earth is definitely ruled by the Kal forces and they will never allow it to happen.

The Kal misleads man. It makes him believe that he can

change the environment and bring about peace and happiness for all mankind. But it is only when man learns to gain control of his own reactions and learns to rule his own inner self that peace and happiness are possible. This is the answer, for he has then accepted individual responsibility for his own reactions and self-control. The other individual has not learned this. Once the chela has grasped this point he has gained great knowledge about entering into the kingdom of Heaven. Unless we have such discipline it is impossible for Soul to travel and explore the spiritual universes, for God leaves all matters of this nature up to the individual.

This being true, there are two things necessary in the ECK chela's training in order for him to enter into the spiritual worlds and enjoy the bliss and happiness that come with his travels. The first of these is that he must never allow mental and emotional conditions to have any power to affect him.

The very thoughts, feelings and emotional outbursts of those occupying space in any given situation in this material universe are apt to affect us in a covert manner that results in outward, or overt, behaviour. Often this goes against our very nature and our relationships with others. This can be in the atmosphere of a room, or in an airport terminal where thoughts pass through daily leaving behind mixed emotions of rage, sorrow, discouragement and other negative feelings. Any sensitive person can pick up these emotional states without knowing it, and react overtly against anyone in his line of fire.

The second aspect necessary to the chela's training is that he must never allow his reactions to these influences to run riot. He must take charge of them. And, to perceive the influence of some negative nature and react to it is not enough. We must learn to counteract it.

The whole process of controlling the environment starts with control of self. Until we cease to be influenced by surrounding conditions, we can never hope to exercise any influence over them. The paradox of this statement is that when we cease to be concerned about the environment, we will have the power to change it.

This is the very reason why the ECK Masters have the power of longevity that staggers the imagination.

The secret of longevity lies deep in the mystery of the human body, in what is known to science as the enzyme. Without enzymes, there is no life. They control all the biochemical reactions of all living things: man, germs, trees and fish. Digestion, breathing, heart pumping, nerve impulses, formation of body tissues, energy to move muscles, growth of the body, all depend upon enzymes.

A single body cell contains up to 100,000 enzymes; each directing a specific action and each coming into play at the right time and place. Until the ECK Masters discovered something about them, few persons, if any, ever lived past the ages of seventy-five to one hundred. But the fact is that most ancient Adepts of the ECK Order of the Vairagi are well into ages beyond the norm of man, in the same continuous body.

Rebazar Tarzs, youngest of the ECK Masters, is said to be over five hundred years old. Fubbi Quantz, head of the Katsupari Monastery in the remote Himalayan mountains of Tibet, is several centuries older than Rebazar Tarzs. Heading the order of the ECK Masters is Yaubl Sacabi, whose age far exceeds any of these just named. Other ECK Masters have kept their physical bodies and are now working on other planets in the universe.

These Masters have learned the secret of enzymes in the human body. They have learned to control them, thus giving themselves mastery over the influence of environment, age and self. They learned long ago that the mere practice of the spiritual exercises of ECK brought results. They know that life is not reduced to the simplicity that the metaphysicians, occultists and religious groups try to teach to the world, like selling a product in modern times to the public.

All of this only affirms the fact that we must change our efforts toward spiritual principles and start from there to control the inner self. No responsibility for any act should be blamed upon another, but accepted fully by ourselves. This is the first ECK principle in seeking self-discipline.

The next step is the practice of the spiritual exercises of ECK, as laid down in Chapter Five. Once we begin working on these, the inner changes start, and our spiritual eye begins to open enough for us to see into the beyond. It is then that we are able to start taking control of our environment. Only through continued practice can we bring ourselves to the point of total control.

To be successful in ECK we must spend more time in diagnosis of ourselves to decide just what action is necessary to bring us the needed self-control. There are several things we can look at that we might be doing that could help us to achieve a better understanding of ourselves. For example: (1) Denial of Reality. Protecting oneself from the unpleasant reality by refusing to face it, by getting sick or occupied with other things. (2) Gratifying frustrated desires in imaginary achievements. (3) Attempting to prove that one's behaviour is rational, justifiable, worthy of self and social approval. (4) Placing blame for difficulties upon others or attributing one's own unethical desires to others. (5) Repression. The preventing of painful or dangerous thoughts from entering the mind. (6) Preventing dangerous desires from being expressed by exaggerating opposed attitudes and behaviour, and using them as barriers. (7) Regression. Retreating to earlier development levels that require less mature responses. (8) Feeling of worth by identifying oneself with persons or institutions of illustrious standing. (9) Covering up weaknesses by emphasizing desirable traits or making up for frustration in some area of emotional life. (10) Discharging pentup feelings of hostility on something that is less dangerous than those who may strike back. (11) Reducing involvement and withdrawing into passivity to protect oneself from emotional injury. (12) Presenting a logic-tight argument against anything that might separate one from his own beliefs and religious attitudes, especially when it seems to be harmful to one's ego. (13)

Bolstering one's ego for self-worth despite failure, by seeking sympathy from others.

These are among the many things that may besiege the chela who wants to look at himself, and learn where his weaknesses might lie. One word of caution, however; the chela should not spend too much time trying to search out his weaknesses. These should be touched upon lightly, then kept in the background so that the chela will not become introverted.

These weaknesses must be initially recognized, then polarized through the spiritual exercises of ECK. It can be done provided the chela keeps at these exercises and does not get discouraged. He also has to recognize that many of the conditions in his life are the result of his karma; he must stop his self-sympathy and resentment of them.

Conditions brought on by karmic debts are experiences to help the chela progress on the spiritual path of development. Once he has given up feeling sorry for himself and has abandoned his resentment against life, he starts breaking the karmic ties that bind him to these situations in life. He begins to work off his karma; he is not subjected to the drastic reactions that come from being initiated too soon, nor to what so often comes should he step off the path of ECK. Unless he has come under the tutelage of the living ECK Master, he could have a rough path to follow.

Too many pseudo teachers and masters initiate their followers on first meeting them only to leave them with their hangups. These hangups are brought into the external with drastic reactions. The poor fellow is usually left with them, suffering through many unnecessary hardships while the leader blithely casts them aside with some vague explanation they are karma.

Do not believe this sort of talk, for the only way one can find peace of mind, rid himself of his karmic debt and take control of himself, is to rid himself of aberrations and other problems through ECK. By his ability to leave this physical state of consciousness and travel into the God states, he can find himself a purified vessel. He can be a channel for God and live in this world of matter while at the same time dwelling in the timeless consciousness.

Within the totality of human experience there have been and are, several kinds of consciousness. Two types of awareness, however, have dominated. They open up different windows of understanding, the one consisting of the Oriental point of view, and the other the Occidental.

Our Western life has tended to concentrate on the outward and active. Our philosophers and intellectuals have striven to find truth primarily through the exercise of reason. In this manner they believe the meaning of the universe can be laid bare. Their eyes are turned to the phenomena of the material world, the nature and laws of which they believe can be discovered through observation, experiment and logical thought. The Westerner's chief object is to control nature via knowledge and bend it to his will. Western history is the story of the conquest of nature by man through reason and science. Thus science and technology have been the achievement of the West.

On the other hand, the Oriental has the tendency to work on the inner self and the passive. He believes that truth cannot be found through knowledge of material phenomena, which is maya, or the appearance of illusion. He seeks truth instead through inner intuition, passivity and contemplation. He feels that human history has little or no meaning, but is only a series of meaningless cycles leading to no goal. Life is a prison from which the enlightened man will, through knowledge of the ECK, escape into the true God realm.

Since we ourselves are instruments for the main body of the highest spiritual ideals known as ECKANKAR, we must be always on the watch in regard to our actions and words. This self-awareness is something that falls in harmony with ECK. It begins to work in a much greater manner with whoever is capable, and ever on the outlook for the deeper and subtler aspects of his own inner self.

As the instrument for this greatest spiritual power within all universes, we must take hold of the basic idea that we are the chosen people. This makes us different from all others in this world, and we must look upon ourselves as heirs to the keys of heaven. We are the kings and queens of the earthly realm, appointed by the divine SUGMAD to take our places here as ITS representatives. We are to act as Godly instruments through which the ECK flows to the world and uplifts humanity.

By divine right we have become the chosen people. And, because we have accepted the responsibility of carrying out the will of God, it is necessary that we have faith and knowledge of being the people of God. Those who do not belong in the spiritual works of ECK have either rejected this path or do not know of it. They will have to wait until the time is ready for each to accept the Mahanta, the living ECK Master.

These people are in a sort of limbo, whether it is in the past or modern times. They will go through lifetime after lifetime wondering why they must suffer, for the Angel of Death does not listen to their cries for mercy but places them back into another life, to pay for their karma.

The Angel of Death is the agent of Kal Niranjan, who is relentless, merciless, and administers absolute justice to each and all, regardless of their position in life. But he who is under the Mahanta's guiding hand will be free of all this; he will be met at the time of death by the living ECK Master and be escorted to the place where he is to enjoy life in the spiritual worlds. He will never have to return again to the physical plane.

By the ECK alone the chela can transcend all lower regions and rise into the heavenly world of the SUGMAD. Without the Mahanta, the living ECK Master, no one can attain conscious union with the stream of pure life, nor can he go further than the first region of light, which is the astral.

Rami Nuri, the great ECK Master in charge of the third section of the Shariyat-Ki-Sugmad, at the Temple of Golden Wisdom on Venus, said, "He who drinks of the stream of ECK can never thirst, but in him is a well of water springing up into life everlasting."

When the chela begins consciously to participate in the

ECK there is within him a well of water ever springing up, sufficient to supply the whole world.

This self-cleansing fountain will go on giving life to every Soul that comes in touch with him. He is now the vehicle of God, the channel for all ECK to flow through and purge all he meets.

Quoting Rami Nuri again, "He who drinks of it will never again search the world looking for food for the inner man. It is there, always within him, the great flowing ECK. It is the SUGMAD shining through him, lighting the world to all who have eyes to see!"

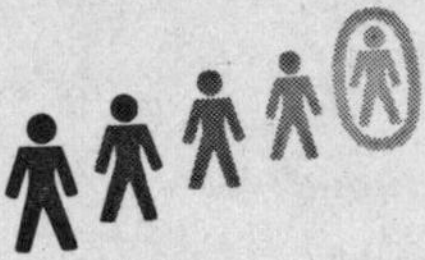

Chapter Eight

THE OBJECTIVE TEACHINGS OF ECK

The problem confronting us all today is a lack of spiritual awareness. But too many people interested in spiritual development seek answers from the field of metaphysics, which creates more problems than it solves. Those instructors who make it sound so simple are hardly any further evolved than the person just beginning his study.

These teachers usually just give the student a full package of intellectual nonsense without telling him exactly what to do with it. This neither resolves problems nor advances the aspirant on the spiritual path. But there are markers along the way for him so that he can constantly check his progress, and this is what will be studied in this chapter.

If a person does not know where he is going, nor even where he is, this is no excuse for him, provided he does not have any spiritual progress. Therefore, it is likely that the agnostic and unbelieving are more blessed than those who prefer to believe. They may have justified their unbelief, but what have these people put their faith into to create such determined wills?

Man's greatest problem is his sensitivity to the indifference of the universe, the alienness of the world around him. One can only wonder at the absurd persistence of human beings whose delusions of grandeur are incurable. It appears to those lost in the human state of consciousness that life is no more than a dream. For those in this state it never becomes a reality.

This sensitivity began its development in man's consciousness during the earlier ages of his time on earth. We think of it first starting in the great empire of MU, which was a part of that lost continent now lying beneath the vast Pacific. It was the largest of all empires this world has ever known, existing some 70,000 years B.C

The great cities of the Gobi desert were part of the empire of MU, located within a vast region of the motherland known as Uighur. It was probably the largest part of the empire, and certainly the greatest this world has ever known. It was the home of the Aryan race and it was here that Yuont-Na, now a teacher of the Shariyat-Ki-Sugmad on the astral plane, was the leading teacher of ECKANKAR.

He lived and taught in the capitol city of Kharahota, which now lies buried deep underneath the sands of the Gobi. Some of the old Naacal records, which are the oldest writings of man and kept in one of the Tibetan monasteries, speak of Yuont-Na and his teachings of the ECK.

The spiritual works of ECK were popular among the upper classes then, especially among a small group who were taught by secret, oral instructions. They acted as a channel for the God force, helping to change the nature of those willing to listen and practice the transcendental exercises of ECK.

Generally speaking, it is a waste of time for any spiritual Master to give out the works of God, and this Yuont-Na soon learned. The great majority of readers and audiences are the same the world over. If the Master speaks to them of profound truths they yawn, and if they dared they would leave the meeting. But if told absurd fables, then they are all ears and sitting on the edges of their chairs.

Yuont-Na realized that audiences wish the doctrines that are preached to them, whether religious, philosophical or social, to be agreeable. They wish them to be consistent with their concepts, and to satisfy their hunger. In fact, they want to find themselves in them, which is to say they feel that any spiritual teaching must be approved personally by them.

So many persons express the desire to find a religious belief that satisfies them. They usually reject some doctrine with the remark, "It does not satisfy me." What is it then that they are seeking in order to become satisfied?

That something which must be satisfied is a collection of false notions and feelings primarily of sensuality. These are disguised under the ego, "I," and manifest as unreasonable

122

attachments to materialities. It rejects anything that does not give them immediate answers nor help at once. But mainly we are dealing with three types of mentality: those with dull intelligence, those with average intelligence, and those with keen intelligence.

The teachings of ECK will always remain secret for individuals with dull minds, who can read and hear what is said to them but cannot grasp anything. Thus the secrecy of the ECK teachings does not depend on the Mahanta, but on the chela. The Mahanta can only open the door; it is for the chela to be capable of seeing what lies beyond that door.

The ECK Master is able to discern the degree of intellectual awareness in those who desire the teachings, and he reserves a more detailed explanation of certain aspects of ECK for those whom he judges able to receive truth. He pours the ideas and principles of ECK into the minds, hearts and Souls of all who come in contact with him, whether it be upon the outer plane or the inner. But it is up to the chela to work with all that is given. The teachings become like a powerful battering ram, for they are not in accord with the false ideas and notions rooted in the mind of man that have before delighted him. Now the false teachings will cast him into suffering.

The point here is that truth, or the ECK, does not cause the chela's suffering; it is the false teachings that resist. Man loves to cling to something, and will happily hold closely to his breast anything that has been 'given him in the past through environment or teachings that might be alien to both his true nature and his spiritual progress, but he accepts them without question. This is what causes the chela's suffering when the ECK appears in his life. The conflict between the two is senseless, for when one keeps clinging to his old ideas the fight is only greater and more prolonged.

I remember an occasion when Sudar Singh spoke about his hesitation before beginning his mission. He said: "I remember well standing in front of an audience that was expecting me to utter profound wisdom, but it wasn't possible.

"The only possible words I could think of at the time were, 'I have discovered a profound truth; difficult to perceive, difficult to understand, and only accessible to the wise.'

"I was aware that Buddha had the same problem during the first few moments of his initial talk on his great mission. I believe that every true spiritual Master who attempts to speak before an audience experiences this same thing time and again, no matter how experienced they are in addressing groups of devotees.

"The wisdom that we all want to speak of and tell others about cannot be expressed with words or deeds. It must be realized. It must be known by others, by those who listen.

"Because people are busy in themselves and find their pleasure in the vortex of the world, it is difficult for men to understand the law of the ECK: that linked series of causes and effects, the holding down of the samskaras; the mental formations, ideas and concepts that depend upon ignorance.

"Then what use is it to reveal to man what any spiritual giant has discovered at the price of laborious effort? Why should I share the fruits of my labor with others who would destroy such at the wink of an eye, or laugh in scorn at my words merely because they furnish them no pleasure for the mind and body.

"I have often wondered why this feeling of compassion for the lost sheep should always be my responsibility. But this doctrine cannot be understood by those filled with worldly desires and unhappiness. ECK is too deep, too mysteriously hidden from the minds of those who carry common thoughts.

"So it was my feeling that I should not proclaim the message of ECK because none would be able to understand it, and the only results would be fatigue and annoyance for me.

"So my first speech to an audience was not really a speech, but an hour of silence. Everyone went away in different states of mind; some confused, others feeling that they had at last come to the right Master because he did not fill them with words they couldn't understand.

"Thus the seeds of wisdom fell somewhat upon barren grounds, except for those few who were able to understand the meaning of silence, who knew that I really had nothing to say because words could not express the reality of the truth I had discovered."

But Sudar Singh was not left without anything to give to the world. At this point the ECK intervened, which put into words the thoughts springing up in his mind and conquered his hesitation to tell audiences the truth of the struggle between the ECK and the Kal. He brushed away the dust that had settled in the spiritual eyes of the ignorant, and broke up the false doctrines that had been spread by so many who had tried to travel the path before him.

When the Master looks over any audience he sees with spiritual eyes those who are able to accept the message of the Sangwa, the secret doctrine of ECK, and those who cannot. He knows that oral teachings are only for those who will understand, who are endowed with a better intelligence than the general masses who gather at such meetings in hopes of finding something that "satisfies" them.

There is nothing in these teachings for the purpose of amusing anyone. They are for the strong to become stronger, for the intelligent to make themselves more intelligent, and to lead each into the transcendent light and sound. These are given instruction in the Temples of Golden Wisdom so they will become the special class, the corps which will be able to understand and accept the true teachings.

The wisdom contained in the Shariyat-Ki-Sugmad is secret, and reserved in the Temples of Golden Wisdom for a certain class of chelas. For this fact alone it is called secret!

The ECK knowledge of the chelas is genuinely of divine inspiration, and dates from the earliest period of history on the planet of Venus. Its teachings are considered to be secret, but are handed down from Master to chela in an uninterrupted line. Those initiated in these secret teachings are well versed in the wisdom of the famed Temples of Golden Wisdom because the living ECK Master sees that they get their spiritual education.

The attainment of illuminated insight is the real goal of those training in the teachings of ECK. The word "teachings" is used often, but actually it is a revelation of certain secrets that also show the chela how to use and discover them for himself.

Since the Mahanta is the Master of the secret teachings, truth learned from any other source is of little or no value. The only truth that is living and effective—that is of value to the chela—is the truth he learns of himself.

Only the living ECK Master is capable enough to give truth as it is to the chela. Unless he is under the ECK Master then his gathering of truth has little value. He is unable to establish any link with the Godhead and, more importantly, is unable to find a way to discover truth for himself. The Master is the link between the chela and the Godhead, for he is the living Word Itself. And he does not work only on the lower planes and planets, but in every plane throughout the universes of God.

The living ECK Master has existed in form since the beginning of all worlds. He comes in every age. There is never a time when he does not exist, since the start of time itself. Only his name and body have changed, and since he is the only living form with a linkup between the entities and material life of all planes, he appears to everything in the very form they recognize.

The basic recommendation the ECK Master gives to the aspirant is to doubt all things, for doubt is the incentive to learn and to understand what is going on in the interworlds. Unless one researches and looks for knowledge, via the ECK Master, it will never be his own.

The chela is never thrown upon his own while traveling the path, though it seems to many that he might be. This is by no means so, for the ECK Master is always standing at his side, gently guiding him and taking him over the obstacles to the Godhead. The path is long and so many times the chela becomes impatient, but he must feel that the Master is always guiding every step of his way into the heavenly worlds.

The chela is put face to face with certain facts, facts which have always seemed so obvious to him that he never gave them a moment's thought. But the ECK Master says, "Take a look at these and examine them carefully, for they are reality. Put aside all preconceived notions, empty yourself of all opinions and take up the study of these facts with doubt in mind. Examine everything about them, including the mental reactions they cause to rise in you."

The world then suddenly becomes transparent. The basic fundamental of life is found, that Reality is equivalent to existence. In other words, that which is real also exists. It is also that which produces effects, because we have a mental and physical reaction to it. We know that certain sensations in the mind and body can arise from a study of certain facts. Therefore we must learn to be wary of the workings of the mentality and the human senses, and then the measurement of our existence in time and space. All this can be gauged in relation to time and space by the mind's reaction to these facts examined.

I have always said that the key to spiritual consciousness lies within each of us. Therefore, we must begin to think about the data in the above paragraph. This could well be the key to open that door of Soul, for many who have been trying for years.

The success of the sea of teachings lies only in the intensity of the contacts made between the ECK and the sense organs of the individual. The impressions received by the physical senses from the inner teachings are fixed upon the mind if they are strong enough in their concentrated force to push through the mind barrier.

We are concerned here with the strength of the impression, or what is known as awareness. For example, if someone looks at a landscape daily but fails to see the topography of trees, hills and grass, his awareness is not strong enough to make him see them consciously. This applies to the inner teachings and especially to Soul Travel.

So many people travel by this method but fail to have any impressions. This is due to the fact that the inner senses did receive some imprint, but not sufficient to hold and become enough aware of to create a memory pattern for the physical sense organs to grasp and retain, and further enable him to describe what happened during his spiritual journey.

Soul can travel in a variety of interesting directions while journeying through the universes. If the entity is concerned with time and space he could get into the Atma plane and take a look at the time track of history. There, if the nature of the ECK were not to unfold Soul into higher ethical standards of conduct, It might try to make a change in the records of human history—which is possible—and create something different today.

Suppose a person wanted to marry a woman who has rejected him and wed another. He wants to travel into the worlds of the beyond and find that region whereby he can control time. He goes backward in time, and comes to the point where he and the young woman were compatible with one another. At this point he is willing to change the whole course of events and keep her from another marriage by making her his spouse. Supposedly they would live happily ever after, then.

However, if one tries to change the course of karma he puts himself in an untenable position. He could take on the karma of the situation or, if he is trying to change an event like Napoleon's march on Moscow, the Lords of Karma may become angry and make him solely responsible for the troubles created by not letting events run their own course. Thousands and even millions of lives were tied up in this particular event of history, for those who marched on Moscow with Napoleon were serving out their own karma. Whoever tried to make a change in order to justify himself runs into the problem of guilt for interfering with the laws of karma, and must pay a severe penalty.

This is a point which the chela must take into consideration when stepping out on the path to God-Realization. He may believe in the beginning that this is possible, but what he forgets is that his values on life will change, and he will no longer try to keep any hold on another person's life. After all, it is the basis of all the ECK work to be detached from an emotional feeling for another person, and from the material things of life.

The next step that the chela must take is to break with his traditional past. Nearly everybody living today in the Western world has accepted Christianity, and those in the Orient have accepted either Hinduism, Buddhism, or one of the six great systems of that world. Naturally, almost everything we have learned has been at our mother's knee, where we were also taught our religious beliefs.

The factor remaining, though, is that every chela will come to a crossroads in his life. This is known as the Bihanwi stage of spiritual development. The word Bihanwi means great crisis in the unfoldment of the consciousness, in spiritual growth. This is when the chela must either break with his traditional religious past and accept ECK as the only force of divine nature, or stay at a standstill in his spiritual growth until he comes to the decision himself.

ECK does not make any break with a traditional religious past, but It does try to get the chela to look hard at it and make his own decision. It realizes that every man in the world must seek the path for himself, and walk upon it himself.

Now that a spiritual darkness broods over the land and all people are sick from it, there is proof that the orthodox religions are not doing much for mankind. Man's great problem is that he has not turned to the ECK Master to receive spiritual redemption.

Religions have been fostered through feelings and metaphysical speculations. And, while each religion serves its purpose in its own time and day, each must eventually give way to something more complete as mankind advances. Hence the ever-recurring need for living ECK Masters. This is the reason why the SUGMAD makes ITS appearance again and again in this world, through the manifestation of the ECK Master.

The chela ascends the inner worlds one after another until he enters Daswan Dwar, that heavenly region beyond the last materialistic plane. Then he beholds himself as pure spirit, stripped of all materiality. This is Self-Realization. After this he advances into the higher regions and beholds the sublime manifestations of God, eventually coming to know God. This is God-Realization.

Anything less than God-Realization is speculative, imaginary, visionary, and imperfect. This would be summing up the beliefs of the mystics, churches, and other forms of outer worship. They all believe that Self-Realization is the ultimate of the Godhead, but the ECK chela is able to reach the God-Realization state via the ECK Master, and can travel anywhere in the spiritual worlds under his direction. Unless the chela has this guidance and protection he will never get beyond the higher astral worlds.

It was a bright sunny day in May, 1527. Rebazar Tarzs was visiting the great oracle of Tirmer in the mountains of northern Tibet, when its voice came ringing down from the mountain peak and across the valleys. "Christ is dead!" the oracle announced clearly. At that very moment the attack of Rome was taking place by Constable duc Bourbon, under Charles V of France. He was trying to topple Clements VII from the papal throne.

Rebazar Tarzs knew what was taking place. The power of the church in the West was broken. In the wake of the oracle's announcement came the schisms that broke up the concentration of the church as a stable force in the lives of all Occidental people. The humanist theory swept across Europe, Martin Luther formed the Protestant church; Henry the VIII broke with the Pope and formed the Church of England; Zwingli, John Calvin and others also broke off from Rome, while inside it men like Savanarola led attacks on the immorality of the official church family.

Due to a lack of leaders to take the place of the founder of Christianity the line had come to a halt with Clements VII, who has never been spiritually replaced. Today the church is like a fish floundering out of water, gasping for breath. Unless the power of the spiritual mantle is handed down from Master to Master, as in the line of ECK Masters, no religion, philosophy or institution can survive. It must have a living Master at the head, or die.

When the teachings of ECK become obscured and corrupt one of the Masters of Its message will show himself in public to straighten out the world matters from the spiritual affairs. Otherwise the ECK Masters keep themselves fairly well hidden from the general public.

The fundamental requirements for meeting a genuine Sat Guru are humility, love, and freedom from the bonds of religions and creeds. The ECK Master always teaches that the Kingdom of God is within man, that whosoever seeks It may find It, but he does more than this: he always shows the chela the exact way to enter that Kingdom. He does this through Soul Travel, and it is for this reason that a living ECK Master is essential.

No matter how great a past Master has been he can neither act in this capacity nor take the chela into the heavenly realm. The chela in a physical body must have a Master in the physical body, one who has the inner freedom to be the ECK Itself, yet also have free movement in all the inner kingdoms of God while his human body works on the human level. This is a fixed law of the SUGMAD. At the time of his passing every Master turns over his work to another Master in the body, who then carries on until it is his time to leave this world.

This is merely the process of the ECK taking up another manifestation of Itself in a physical form. Because the physical body and senses are subject to the law of life and death in this universe, the ECK can use a human vehicle for only so long. Then It will leave that form and take up residence in another. Usually the ECK Master does not die, in the same way we know human death, but merely moves out of this arena of action into another. The living ECK Master turns over the Rod of Power to his successor at a particular time and then withdraws into the other worlds. Sometimes he stays around, like Rebazar Tarzs, Fubbi Quantz and Yaubl Sacabi.

These beings have passed through the state of Mahanta-ship, which is the highest spiritual consciousness one can attain in this world. A number of letters pass through this office from those who request an audience with Rebazar Tarzs and other ECK Masters, but they do not understand that these great Souls have succeeded in their spiritual missions here and have left the physical worlds, in a sense, and become mighty beings. One cannot have a physical audience with any of them, but can see, talk, and be advised by any provided he is able to see them with spiritual eyes.

At this point we must enter into the absolute truth. Up to this time the chela has dealt mostly with dreams, images and mirages. The teachings of the religionists have their followers believing in dead images, those which have been but are no longer. In other words, what we usually see are the images of dead things.

These are called dead because they are images of the past. William Blake wrote of this in his famous poem, Jerusalem, when he described the Hall of Los where the events of our lives are all gathered in the form of statues. Only spotlighting our attention upon them gives them life. This is the dead image, the events that are made by the karma of today and of the future; the part of our lives that comes out of the past, into the present, and shapes our lives today.

Viewed thus, an Akashic reading is scarcely more than a scanning of dead images to find something that has already existed, and perhaps made our lives what they are today. This is something few, if any, spiritual seekers want for themselves. What they are interested in is the live image.

What then is the live image? It is the image that the chela sees beyond the physical senses. It is not a vision, nor something conjured up in the imagination, but it is seeing reality for what it is with the spiritual eyes. It is not seeing into the future, nor looking at the past, but it is seeing and knowing the forces and currents that are always swirling around one. To know and understand these undercurrents, and to see clearly the pictures of the spiritual world, is to have reality in one's life.

Then we learn that theories and doctrines of all kinds are

but fabrications of the mind. We must be careful of this fabricating ability for the resultant theories are misleading and can take us in the opposite direction of the God realm.

The pure image is very clear. It is reality of itself, and in it the chela will have varied experiences that do not come with false imagery. In the pure image one is able to see, know, have all the perceptions of color, smell, taste, hearing and feeling. This all comes through the spiritual eyes.

There is a certain perceptiveness that comes with pure imagery which is unexplainable. One must accept this because it involves the understanding and knowledge that the law itself works differently in the spiritual worlds than in the psychic. And, it is the working of the spiritual law that must be taken into consideration.

We must either accept or deny the imagery that takes place within our own world. If we are perceptive enough we can grasp that this imagery is outside our own world, in what is called the universal world. The difference here is between the personal universe and the cosmic universe, but once this is understood we can find the difference between the two and save ourselves a terrible amount of trouble.

This is the downfall of those psychics who predict earthquakes, wars, and other disasters that affect mankind. Unknowingly they fall under the illusion of seeing a crackup in their own universe and mistake this for a universal disaster. They create panic among those who are gullible enough to believe such prophecies. The whole problem, though, is that the crackup in their own universe, which they witnessed, could be an indication of the splitting of their own personality, which leads to serious mental conditions.

There is a terrible struggle going on constantly between the worlds of imagery and the worlds of psychiatry and psychology. The battle is fiercest fought between the spiritually minded and the sophisticates. The latter are the so-called realists who try to drive followers of the spiritual path insane. If we are watchful, though, there is no need for this to happen to any chela traveling the path of God.

Because of this I will build an entire new world that is

believable. The facts of pure imagery, or what we call reality, must become as acceptable to us as the facts of the physical senses. Therefore, no chela on the path of ECK should allow himself to fall into this lower state. If he does his work must be done all over again. He must know and understand that the basis of spiritual law is that when one is dwelling in the higher worlds he is a law unto himself. Because pure imagery is his experience he is welcome to accept or reject it, for this is the crux of the spiritual life. We become the law of ourselves and therefore must make our own decisions, have faith in what we experience, and know that this is right. Until we accept this basic fact of ECKANKAR we will not succeed in life in any manner whatsoever.

Once we establish this principle in our lives we suddenly discover that there is a control over all things. This could be known as the "as if" principle, meaning that all manifestation can be brought to its last stage of illusion by simply accepting pure imagery as the final analysis. Then the chela can direct this imagery to create the condition desired and keep its behaviour under control. The ECK Master teaches the chela to act "as if" he has already achieved the states desired in the higher consciousness.

The ECK is an invisible current, running through the life of each man. If the physical form, sensation, perception, mental activity and consciousness are taken away from the individual one wonders what remains of him. Where do we find man existing outside himself?

Frankly, we do not find him. What we have just taken away from man is his ego; the part of him that makes up the negative consciousness, or the negative self that we call human nature. The secret wisdom puts emphasis upon doing away with this human nature, in a manner of speaking, and taking on a new self, or the spiritual nature. In the absence of the human self, then, the inner self stands forth and sees all with spiritual sight, and understands all with spiritual knowledge.

The ego, human nature, is sustained by a continuous flow or succession called Santana, in the Sanskrit tongue. It simply means the continued flow of a stream, and when applied to man it means the stream fed by karmic activities. Once the individual starts out on the path of ECK the karmic pattern, or rather the Santana, will gradually start to dry up like the waters of a creek in hot weather. The good deeds performed in the service of the Mahanta do not feed this steady karmic flow, whereupon it can no longer exist.

At the present, humanity appears like a procession of ants laboring to carry off some object to its own nest. When the individual rises out of this parade of mankind and into the higher realms he drops all racial, national and familial karma, and his own personal karma starts working itself off. He begins to find his own identity for the first time in many lifetimes. This is what the Tibetans called the chain of originations. Once the initial cause is created the effects are likely to run throughout the lifetime of the individual and into centuries of future lives.

The most striking facet of the ECK teachings is that which concerns going beyond this state. This involves entering into the depth of wisdom; the best, highest, secret wisdom of all things. The terminology used mostly by the Tibetans actually describes the phase of life that shows us the spirit behind all life. This is in effect the whole of the secret doctrine of ECKANKAR.

Those with little knowledge seem to think that life ends in the astral worlds, those with some knowledge think that life gains itself in some sort of realization in the mental worlds, and those with a greater knowledge than either of these believe that the Atma plane, or the fifth world, is the end of all things. They believe that Sat Nam is God Itself. They have little logic to determine that beyond lies all of the Absolute Reality.

These are all merely states of consciousness that have not yet reached the greater spiritual unfoldment of life. Soul is destined to go beyond wisdom-knowledge. When the ECK Masters decide that an individual Soul has fulfilled Its places in the study of the Shariyat-Ki-Sugmad in the Temples of Golden Wisdom, then it begins to reach out into the worlds beyond-the-beyond. The living ECK Master encourages It to travel as far as It possibly can, according to the spiritual unfoldment It has at that particular time. One must remember that no Soul can go beyond its own capacity, beyond its own growth. If It should do so tremendous problems would occur which would not be natural and might bring about a relapse, or at least a halt in the Soul's progress.

The chela must become an initiate before he can start going into the higher worlds. He must pass the first initiation, then go through two or three more before establishing himself in the true spiritual worlds and using them as a base from which to work. This is the liberation, the salvation of Soul. It is also called Moksha, that is, the liberation, or more often the Jivan Mukti, which means spiritual liberation during this lifetime. While he lives in the spiritual worlds in Soul form, he also lives in a physical body in the material worlds, and he is able to function in both bodies at the same time.

Someone like the living ECK Master is able to live in two or more bodies at the same time. This is not uncommon, and although seldom practiced, it is not impossible to find him operating one physical body in one place and perhaps a thousand miles away be running another physical form also.

In the East it is not unusual to find many who believe that by dying they are "going west," an expression that gained some prominence during World War 1. The mystics always use the symbolic east, where the sun rises daily, to say that life begins in the resurrection. Some say they are going south into life, but it is generally by going north that the symbolic expression of life is found. This is because north of India lies Tibet and the mighty Himalayan mountains.

This is what is meant when the ECK Master says we must travel for a long time before reaching the Godhead, for what he is saying is that the secret teachings lead one on the long hard path. But when asked, "Does it lead to the goal of God," he only smiles and remains silent.

Eventually the Godhead or realm of God is abandoned as

a final, absolute objective, for every saviour, every saint and every master knows there is a plus element in the spiritual worlds. We never reach that state of ultimate perfection for which the mystics always long. Perfection is always one step beyond the last one, and he who has a deep wisdom of God knows this. Therefore he is always contented with what he has until the next level is ready for his unfoldment.

This "beyond-the-highest" stage of God-Realization is associated with non-activity. Deliverance into the true realm of heaven is sometimes sudden and startling, but mostly it is a gradual growth so Soul can become used to every step and adjust naturally. Liberation is achieved by the practice of non-activity, which is sitting still and doing something.

The teachings are not meant to invoke any particular feelings. The living ECK Master expects the chela to examine the questions to which his attention has been drawn, and find reasons there for a serene indifference. He learns that dislike is a form of attachment turned upside down, and that both have the same effect of binding the person who feels them to the particular object or person. He must play out the game of life, be it comedy or drama, until he at least understands that it is all a game.

All in all he must learn to look with the same serene indifference at both the incessant workings of his mind and the physical activity displayed by his body. He will learn that nothing of all that comes from him is really himself. He is only physically and mentally the composite of all the things going on within him. The serene, indifferent self is the true self, Soul.

CHAPTER NINE

THE SUBJECTIVE TEACHINGS OF ECK

Whenever a chela considers his subjective world—like the mental plane—he finds a multitude of other beings, including many of his contemporaries. These consist of people with whom he associates, communicates, and whose actions he both watches and participates in as a group.

While the individual absorbs both the positive and negative energies of these people he is constantly coming into contact with, a continual inhibition is at work. These energies, alien to his own powers, often install themselves in his mental self, which is the ego or "I." There they form a swarming throng of selves, which in turn make up conflicting opinions, ideas and beliefs.

These other egos become guests in the individual's mental world and often create problems. It does not matter whether they are in books, on the screen, or actual persons, these egos become part of his own makeup and wield influence over him and the world about him. Some of them actually belong to the past, and could include Buddha, Plato, Jesus, Rousseau, Napoleon, Columbus, Jefferson and Lincoln, to name only a very few.

These egos become a problem because Soul, while encased in the body, gets too blind in the physical world to do much about them. Each of the above named represents a diversified crowd who are forceful, turbulent, and thirsting for prestige. Each will try to impose the repetition of his own physical and mental image upon the reader, or one who tries to accept them into his own mental world. It is not the message they left to the world, but the image established through the years that is implanted upon the minds of the individual trying to do research or studying their works and biographies.

When the chela becomes aware of the throng of personalities within himself, he should not indulge in any imagination that they represent memories of his past lives. One of the gross misunderstandings of many chelas is that they are reincarnations of famous persons out of the past. This misunderstanding arises from a wrong interpretation of the swarming crowd within themselves. The Asiatics will often conjure up such stories among the masses in hopes of bringing about miracles and marvelous happenings.

The teachings of ECK prove that there is quite a difference between reincarnation and the crowd of personalities that become part of the memories and mental world of the individual. The energies these living beings set in motion were only the manifestation of multiple energies. Each within themselves, like Jesus or Aristotle, was the manifestation of these living entities before them, whose ancestry came out of the unfathomable depths of eternity.

Thus the individual chela who comes to the living ECK Master is filled with these living presences also. He is the center for these beings, unconsciously of course, until the living ECK Master begins to take these entities out of him and make him strictly an autonomous individual. He then is purified to be a clear channel for God.

It is a principle of ECK to break up these beings in the chela and allow him to be himself. None of the swarm of personalities have any further power over him once he steps into the world of ECK. In Tibet the Dalai Lamas, leaders of the Buddhist sect, are called the living Buddha. This means each is a reincarnation of another previous individual, and so into the past, forming reincarnations to some prominent person who began the line. This happens in families, groups, and even business lines.

Thus we find a definite problem arising. The forces combine in the manifestation of a singular individual, one or several of them together, and aim at a goal unattainable in the lifetime of the person involved. This is the crux of the matter in which those who preach God-Realization are wrong. Due to these circumstances and other multiple problems, the individual is not likely to be at the stage of spiritual unfoldment in which Self-Realization is possible, much less God-Realization.

Therefore the metaphysicians' and religionists' theory that we are able to reach God in one lifetime is only a general hypothesis. It is an academic idea, but once the chela understands this swarming throng within himself then he begins to know the truth about ECKANKAR. It is the only path he can take which will sweep these personalities out of him and make him a clear channel. No other path will do so.

It follows that if Abraham Lincoln and others continue their lives in any person or number of persons, then these recipients have no authority to claim they are Lincoln or any other reincarnated personality. Only a fraction of these personalities re-live in the individual. Sentiments transmitted by means of reading or speeches are needed to call up the thoughts, words and deeds of these eminent personalities, in order to bring out the characteristics of one personality who lived in the past.

This is why I have often stated that one should give up studying other works too much while on the path of ECK. The chela trying to express himself becomes only a mouthpiece for an entity who had a physical life once and left behind his philosophy at that time. The chela could thus become a clear channel for something other than the SUGMAD, for any entity wanting to use him for its own purpose could crowd out the others and make itself prominent in his life. We in ECK are more interested in seeing the chela become himself, rather than someone else.

This is why the ECK Master will never interfere in the affairs of a chela. He wants him guided so that he develops his own personality. In the beginning there is a certain amount of reading done, but then the chela should stop it and bring himself to studying nothing but ECK. This will lead him towards being a clear channel for God.

All this lies in the area of attitude. The chela must at all times be faithful to the cause of ECK. If he is not then he is defeating himself and is left without defense against the swarm of entities within him. These swarms misrepresent themselves to spiritualists, those who depend upon mediums to link them up with disembodied spirits. Entities who have long been deceased will speak through the medium to its recipient. Some of these entities will say they are Jesus, Mohammed, Buddha, or dozens of other prominent historical figures.

These are not entities playing tricks on the recipient, as many who are enemies of spiritualism claim. But they are some of the inner throng who have become a part of that individual during past lives, or within this present life. Also, and most importantly, they are within the medium, and unconscious as he may be of this phenomenon, they use him to get their specific message across. This might be compared to circuits, or valences. The word is not to be confused with the same used in chemistry, but a valence is a proven affinity between two terminals, two entities or lines of power, outside the individual and within him.

Neither is this to be confused with any aspect of mental health. The entities placed within the individual during his lifetimes, through certain lines of force, depend on several things.

First is religious background. If the individual is a Christian, then the line of force belonging to Jesus will be stronger in him. If he is an Easterner, the Buddha, Krishna, or some other traditional religious deity within that world will be the line of force. This is learned from childhood, usually before the age of six. This is the proper place to start developing the lines of power, or entities within the person.

Second, after having been implanted with an entity of this nature, the individual will find it grows within him according to how it is nurtured. For example, having been raised as a Christian, he supplements his early knowledge of Jesus by reading and attending church regularly, until the entity crowds out most of the others within the individual's life.

Third, the individual is unable to get rid of this entity because the more he strives to do so, the more it becomes implanted within him. When anything like a brainwashing job is done on him to change his thought patterns and ideals in life, it is generally a failure. That is, unless the individual undergoing this sort of treatment desires to make the change.

Those who wish to control the minds of others fail to see something that is vastly more important than brainwashing. Not having any knowledge of psychic phenomena they run into a barrier when they think that all attitudes, thought patterns and ideals have been washed out of the individual undergoing change by their methods.

Freud was wrong in his theory and so was Pavlov. Both used specific techniques to change the basic structure of man's thinking. They were relatively successful at this, but not in changing the basic nature of the individual. No psychological method, no amount of physical torture and no materialistic or mental control can defeat the swarm of entities within the individual.

There is an exception to this rule. When the traditional home training of the individual is neglected, then this can come about. Also, when some entities of the internal throng are already stronger in the direction in which he is being indoctrinated, then the person will more easily be brainwashed.

There is a struggle here between the ECK and the individual who wants spiritual works but cannot give up that last traditional value established within him. The swarm of entities we have been speaking about refuse to let go. They will fight desperately to the last ounce of strength to hold on to their channel into this world.

The crux of the visions and insights that saints, mystics and holy men write of so much is scarcely more than the visitation of these entities. They make themselves known to saints and others who dwell mainly in the visionary fields. Then he who has the greatest traditional strength within the individual will appear and give messages, dialogues; will heal, guide, and bring about certain forms of illusions which are always encouraged by the Kal force, until the individual actually believes what he thinks has been witnessed.

Tradition, coupled with faith in some religion which has strong images of the founder of the apostles firmly established in the minds of the masses, makes it possible for these entities to break through the barriers into the open. This is a wrong way to attempt spiritual unfoldment of anyone. It causes a seed to be implanted in the deeper self which cannot be broken until the aspirant rises above the physical and psychic planes. Once he is able to do Soul Travel and reach into the higher worlds then this swarm of entities will leave. No longer can they be a part of him for he breaks with his past, and his karma, as well as his future, travels a smoother road.

As an example of these entities, let us take a look at Shakespeare. The role of Hamlet is an exceedingly hard one for any actor. The challenge is often beyond the endurance of whoever attempts it. It is known that those who play this role, or any other part in the tragedy, come to grief or bad luck. It is such a challenge though that few consider this when offered parts in the play. This is true also of Shakespeare's famous tragedy Macbeth.

Such is the thread that runs deeply in the character of every living person. We must remember that those who have passed on into the next life are unable to act as transformers in the physical for those still living there. This is a grave error made by so many people today. They hold the illusion that a person who has died and is now living in the astral or other psychic worlds, including the spiritual, can give them direct assistance.

This is not true, however, for they have no physical vehicle through which to work. Every individual living here must use the physical body as his instrument to express that which comes from the beyond. Every Soul leaving the physical body at death must use the body of whatever plane he goes to, be it the astral, causal, mental or etheric. He becomes the instrument of God on the plane he dwells upon, but he cannot express himself through the body or vehicle of another person who is living on the physical, or any other plane. Only the living ECK Master can do this, for he is spiritually developed so that he can act as the instrument of God on any plane, as long as he retains a physical body.

144

When the ECK Master leaves this plane he is not capable of being a channel for the physical world, but his successor takes up the responsibility. Thus the ascended Masters have little power in this physical plane. This must be understood by the chela because it is very important.

Only the living ECK Master assumes the duty of being both the outer and the inner Master. It is for this reason that some ECK Masters retain their bodies so long in this universe. These particular saints of ECKANKAR are staying here for a purpose: to act with the living ECK Master and those who are able to work into their orbit. They will never bypass the living ECK Master, though, for he has been given the Rod of ECK power and supersedes all others in heaven and earth, until the time of either his passing from the worldly body or his retirement in the physical form to do spiritual work.

Whoever accepts the Rod of ECK power becomes the Mahanta. This is a spiritual title designating the highest state of consciousness while still in this world and carrying on the duties of the living ECK Master. It has been passed down for centuries upon centuries from the time of the first ECK Master and Mahanta, to the present. Each who has the title of Mahanta is the divine manifestation of God. It is his duty and responsibility to take those Souls who are ready and have been prepared back to the Godhead for permanent residence.

It is for this reason that ECK has nothing to do with the second coming of Christ, as explained in Christianity, nor the Mitreya, which is the return of the Buddha, in the East. Other religions, too, have been seeking the return of the Messiah within their orb of belief, that they may have peace and happiness once again upon this earth.

The Egyptian Pharaoh of that ancient land was both a god and the son of a god. Everything in the life of Jesus is told also in the life of Krishna, saviour of the Hindu religion. Countless men have become gods, through realization of the Godhead, and innumerable gods have also become men. The sun gods of Asia were given the title of Christ, for it is an ancient title among peoples of the prechristian era. We find saviour gods in various religions, such as Osiris, in Egypt; Mithra, in Persia; Adonis, in Greece; and Attis, in Phrygia. They lived, preached their message, died a violent death and alike were resurrected.

It is interesting that the ECK never bothers with large numbers of people. To understand this we must look at the limitations of consciousness in men. This consciousness which we must concern ourselves with is the materialistic nature.

It is puzzling that the individual should believe that materiality is the whole essence of spiritual works. Naturally, he is far from being right, for this is on the negative end of the polarity, in other words, it is the polarity of the Kal.

For example, a person wanting an initiation in ECK asked if she must give up cocktails, for she had visitors quite frequently who indulged in alcoholic drinks. She believed that it was imposing on her to give up this habit. As far as I was concerned it made little difference whether she did or not. But what became clear was her attitude that this was more important to her than ECK.

This is the most important point that the chela can take up at this level. How far is he willing to go for ECK? No matter how much I write or speak it makes little difference if the chela is not willing to sacrifice for the sake of a greater principle. Most chelas approach ECK with hopes for what It can do for them. This is a very common attitude, for few understand that they must work for and with God, and not the reverse. Pampering the human ego is the greatest error the metaphysicians and religionists have created over the centuries. Everyone is looking to God for help, and never in terms of what can be done for God.

This is materialism at its worst. It is a popular psychological theory started in the nineteenth century aimed at health and wealth and. peace of mind. The middle class has been the target of this new concept, started somewhat by Freud, Phineas Quimby, George Berkley, Bergson and others; only to be carried on by Mary Baker Eddy, Norman Vincent Peale and many branches of New Thought as well as East Indians who came to this country with success-bringing promises of the positive thinking philosophy. Faith healers, psychic readers, and leaders in the health, wealth and peace of mind field have sprung up like weeds.

This is what causes the struggle when the ECK comes out again as the true message of the SUGMAD. Everyone who is concerned first about their health, pocketbook, or peace of mind comes to ECK for repairs. But when they reach that state in their spiritual unfoldment when affairs seem to go wrong they immediately get off the path and head for something else. What they forget is that by entering onto the path of ECK their karma is speeded up. They will therefore have all sorts of problems which must be broken through, for this is the last incarnation they are going to spend on Earth.

When they come to that last step of giving up what stands between themselves and God it is likely they will give up ECK. This has happened time and again. It means they are still in the materialistic world and want nothing but attachments to things that give them the ease and comfort of human life. It is an old trick, unknown to the individual but well known to the Kal, to try and prove a mundane point with the spiritual works of ECK. One is advised not to try this for he will meet with failure everytime he attempts it.

The next thing we meet on the path of ECK is viewing things as a void. The meaning of this word is emptiness in its own nature, being devoid of self-distinctiveness and independent from the elements which compose it. This makes it perceptible, active and efficient. It is different from nothingness. An individual cannot be explained as having nothing because he has all the elements that make up an ego and personality. But the term void is different.

The void has a relative meaning. All that exists has relation to something else; it is fastened to something else and exists only because of this. The void, however, is really a blank, for there is nothing else in relation to it. It is in a sense the original place of all things. Therefore, everything else is relative to It, but It is not in relation to other things. It is what we know in ECK as the Ocean of Love and Mercy, and must be impressed upon the chela as such.

This Ocean of Love and Mercy is a state in which no combination of things can be produced and no phenomenon is possible. It is a state in which only a force, subtle and non-manifest, exists. This force is called the SUGMAD, and Its child, offspring or essence whatever we want to call It is the spirit, or ECK. It is this ECK that creates life and worlds. Being the sphere of a complete absence of any sort of manifestation, it is impossible to conceive of this Void. This is discussed in the first section of the Shariyat-Ki-Sugmad, called the Book of the Tuza (The Book of Soul).

The interesting part of this, according to the Shariyat-Ki-Sugmad, is that the origin of manifestation is not in any place or moment of past time, but it is here and now, produced each instant in the mind of the chela. Every moment of the twenty-four hours, a subjective image of the world as we conceive it rises in our minds, only to sink back again and be resolved in the next instant. It is like the waves that arise in mid-ocean only to fall away into it once more.

All this goes beyond the swarm of entities spoken about earlier in this chapter. When the chela comes to this understanding in his spiritual unfoldment he learns not to be controlled or impressed by these entities. He learns that this place of God, orReality, is his true home, and it is free from any entities or psychic and materialistic things. The chela becomes liberated and will never again return to these worlds of physical and psychic matter.

This is the breaking away of ego, which is the illusion of the lower worlds. It is an awakening that is salvation. ECK proposes no other object than this for the chelas. When one has been awakened he is no longer a believer in the little "I," the ego of the person, and it is at this time that he rejects all beliefs, and is able to distribute the gifts of the SUGMAD.

Characteristics formed by karma are weakened, and begin to drop away little by little in the prolonged course of the spiritual exercises of ECK. The chela will find himself on a clear path, making his way through the relative world, traveling in the worlds of reality, and eventually into that Void we know as the Godhead.

He who is ignorant and dwelling in the worlds of matter sees only suffering and the painful round of deaths and successive births with all that they imply. The Master is free from all entanglements of the lower worlds that could interfere with the message of the ECK, and he knows and relaxes in the world of God. He has long since been awakened and living in the heavenly worlds, while at the same time using his physical form as the instrument through which the ECK force flows to the outer worlds.

Thus what man has wrought belongs in the psychic worlds and what God has wrought belongs in the spiritual worlds. For example, moral law, which is an astral law, rests on the fact that it is possible for every person to develop in a greater degree only emotionally, since emotion is the principle upon which the astral plane is based. It says that man may seek to order his life and relations with others on the basis of love and power. And this is the whole conflict of the astral law of moral purpose. The two forces are antithetical to one another, insofar as it is impossible to spiritually develop in both directions at the same time. When we develop our capacity for power we weaken our capacity for love and, conversely, to the extent that we grow in our ability to love we disqualify ourselves for success in power.

The humanists say that the force of love will triumph over power but this is not true. In reverse they say that the force of power will subjugate love in human relations. Neither of these is actually true. The humanists also claim that love is good and power is bad. Yet this is not strictly a spiritual subject, but one belonging to the astral world. We must consider then that it is a psychic law we are dealing with and not anything on the higher levels of life.

Most of the world's great men have worked with this law to increase their social, political and economic leadership. The extreme ends of human experience in love and power have been Jesus and Hitler, but all their positions really es-

149

tablished were the good and bad extremes of human experience. But we are dealing now with astral laws and that means the former position is taken, for man attempts to establish holes of oblivion in the universe through which all deeds, good and bad, may disappear. This has been a colossal error throughout all history.

We try not to get sociological in order to prove the point between love and power, but we do take the stand that love is emotional force and power is a force of will. How high do they go in man's life? Only to the next plane, and any person who uses either as a sole lever to get himself higher into the worlds of God will certainly determine his own spiritual progress. If he is only willing to reach the astral plane and accept that as his spiritual fulfillment then he should be contented to use love and power as his motivation. But then again he is limiting himself to very little progress on the path of ECK, for his true goal should be that of God-Realization and nothing else.

The fundamental issue involved here with ECKANKAR is essentially about the nature of the conditions governing man's life and welfare. Closely related to and rising out of this problem are the five perversions of the mind which create the conditions of man's life here. These always bring about personal dissatisfaction in the material world and result in the question, "Who am I?"

If the individual is traveling the path of love he is apt to ask this universal question of himself. But if he is traveling the path of power he thinks in terms of "What am I?" Either way these questions are not much good for anything except introversion.

These two questions the chela asks himself are basic in the spiritual life, but he must learn that a final reply does not come with the asking of them. When we speak of the spiritual nature of man, we speak of something above the material aspirations of the individual. The schism that arises between himself as a human and as a spiritual self is extremely important. Which is he going to put first?

The answer is neither. He should really think in terms of

fitting, or putting together, the two selves. They fit like a glove on the hand. While living in this world in the physical body it is imperative that we use the human self while developing the higher abilities of our spiritual side. It is necessary that one augment the other and vice versa.

Therefore we find that ECKANKAR is for the minority—those who are neither the intellectuals nor the masses. Its works are for the special few who are willing to give up everything in Its behalf. The busy, the thinkers and the wealthy, will have difficulty following ECK because of their involvement with the lower worlds. As Rebazar Tarzs once said,"He who follows the senses, he who is interested in business, and he who is interested in guarding his wealth shall never see heaven."

Then who shall see heaven?

Only those who accept God in their life. Those who follow the Mahanta and seek Reality through the path of ECKAN-KAR. Every chela on this path understands that the living ECK Master is the light-giver, or the transformer through which he must go in order to find God. Unless he does this it is impossible to reach the heavenly worlds. He is the only one ever manifesting in all history in whom individualism and universalism are combined in their full expression.

The living ECK Master stands alone; he is a law unto himself. He does as he pleases, has what he wants, comes and goes absolutely at his own will, and asks no favor of any man. Neither does anyone hinder him in the execution of his will, for he has all things at his own command. If he suffers hardships or inconveniences, it is because he chooses to do so for some reason of his own. He is the supreme giver, but not a receiver, for he always pays for what he gets. He does not work by time nor is he bound by any rule or custom outside of himself. He is a citizen of the whole world. His great love alone binds him to all persons and all living creatures. He is the Master of all men and at the same time the servant of all men, but never fettered by human bonds. He severed all human bonds before becoming the Master, yet never does he shirk a duty, nor fail any obligations. His love is one of complete detachment, and in loving this way he gives greater love to all persons. Many feel that he loves them personally, with a warm, personal love, for it is their opinion that he and they have served together in past lives. These persons try to reduce his love for them to a personal, human level, but never does he give affection, only love. Neither does he ask others to make him the object of their affections, but to give him a detached love.

The Master has been with every chela since the beginning of time upon this Earth, and with the other planets and the beings on those worlds. He has assumed another embodiment with each life spent in these worlds. It has always been the ECK which has brought about the existence of the Living ECK Master upon this planet and other worlds. It has only changed forms and handed down Its power from one departing Master to his successor.

The departing Master always leaves on our calendar date of October 22nd, and in turn his successor always accepts the Rod of ECK Power on the same day, at midnight, in the full of the moon in the Valley of Shangta, in northern Tibet, near the Katsupari Monastery. The ritual takes place at the site of the ancient Oracle of Tirmer under the direction of the ancient sage Yaubl Sacabi, whose age is beyond the imagination of the normal senses.

The Adepts of the ancient Order of the Vairagi meet at the time of the handing of the mantle of spiritual power from the departing Master to his successor. These are the well known ECK Masters who are the guardians of the Shariyat-Ki-Sugmad in the Temples of Golden Wisdom, e.g., Fubbi Quantz, Abbot of the Katsupari Monastery; Yaubl Sacabi, supernatural leader of the spiritual city of Agam Des; Rami Nuri, Temple of Golden Wisdom, Venus; Gopal Das, astral plane; Shamus-i-Tabriz, causal plane; Towart Managi, mental plane; Lai Tsi, etheric plane and Ju Chiao, Soul plane.

All the rulers of the various inner planes send their chief representative to this ceremony to greet the living ECK Master who takes the Rod of Power and the spiritual title of Mahanta. Afterwards the ECK Master is greeted by each of these rulers within the worlds of God, as he makes his first official journey through them.

Besides these, the nine secret ECK Masters who are responsible for the hidden knowledge of the spiritual worlds pay homage to the new living ECK Master. These Masters are responsible for the collection of the secret knowledge and its placement into the greatest of sacred books, the Shariyat-Ki-Sugmad.

The living ECK Master then takes up his duties in this world, to serve humanity and gather up as many Souls as possible to return them to the heavenly world. His duties are not with reform nor social activities, nor anything within the society of men, although he is an ideal citizen and willing to exert himself for those who need him in this manner. Still, he has nothing to do with this part of life. He is only interested in the spiritual welfare of man, whom he hopes will turn to him during this lifetime and be taken back to his true spiritual home before physical death.

The Master is never given to ascetic practices, nor unreasonable austerities. He insists that everyone should give attention to the health of the body and mind. Anyone given to self-torture or to self-indulgence is not a Master. Nor does the Master ever ask for a living: he earns his own way and will likewise not allow his chelas to be idle while someone else supports them.

The Master will never perform miracles for public exhibitions. He may do them on special occasions, and for particular reasons, but it is usually kept a secret from the public. It is a law among the ECK Adepts of the Order of Vairagi that they never do miracles to win disciples. The lower masters and teachers may do miracles, heal the sick and other things, but the ECK Masters will never do them, except on certain very special occasions and for very urgent reasons.

The first duty of the ECK Master is to link up Souls with the ECK sound current. He does not do this miscellaneously, like so many others try to do, through initiation. Every chela must prove himself in ECKANKAR. This is because many are called but few are chosen. Knowing this, the Master will be careful to whom he gives an initiation in ECKANKAR, and not allow anyone to take it unless he feels certain they are ready.

Secondly, the living ECK Master must teach the Way to the initiates, who are now considered his disciples. Since there is only a small group who really knows the way through initiation, they have the greater opportunity to become teachers within the works of ECK. The Master alone holds the key to the Kingdom of Heaven for all, but with his disciples come many opportunities to gather up Souls who are wandering along the way. Without the Master no Soul can find his way out of the circle of births and deaths. He may gain either the first or second regions on the pathway to heaven, but there he becomes fixed and unable to move any further. None but the living ECK Master knows the way beyond that, and his wisdom and personal help is essential.

The Master's greatest role is that of redeemer, liberator of all Souls from the eternal wheel, but he is also a teacher. He gives instruction in the science of Soul Travel, which no book can ever reveal.

The living ECK Master is the examplar of the light and sound of God. His primary function is to bring light and love into the world so that all persons may benefit from these wondrous aspects of the SUGMAD. This does not mean that his chelas alone will have the benefits of the inner light and sound flowing through them, but the whole world shall profit thereof by his presence.

This is part of the secret work that he does. No one has the privilege of following him into the secret chambers of his sanctuary and see all the intricate parts of the great work he is doing. His special work is with the chelas, but he also works for all mankind. There is not a living creature or being in the worlds of God who does not receive spiritual benefits from the living ECK Master, including every individual on this and other planets; the constellations and galaxies in the universe. This takes in many spiritual planes beyond the material universes.

Sometimes people criticize the Master for not presenting

visible proof of what he is doing, but they are not aware that he often halts destructive earthquakes, disasters which would upset the world population. But he never takes credit nor shows outwardly that it was his efforts that saved perhaps millions of lives.

He increases the totality of light and sound and love in the world, and every living thing receives benefits from this. One does not have to think about what method he uses but simply looks to the illumination and blessings that the world receives through him.

The Master is used by the SUGMAD to bless the world, and whatever comes into the life of the chela should be interpreted as his own personal benefit for spiritual unfoldment.

CHAPTER TEN

THE PATHS TO GOD AND HOW TO COMPARE THEM

No man, nor any group dwelling within the material universe, has the capacity to encompass God. For that matter, neither has anyone on any plane within the universes of the SUGMAD. Strange as this may sound it is true, for not even the saviours or saints have developed that capacity of consciousness.

We are faced here with the fact that there is always a plus element in purification. No being has ever reached the state of perfection so often promised and described by the religionists. It is utterly impossible, for God is so immense that we have not the imagination to conceive this unlimitedness. If one can think of eternity and have the least conception, get even the tiniest glimpse of it, then it is possible to get the large view of God. But not the complete concept.

The capacity to accept God into one's life is very small regardless of what we might believe. Yet so many teachers and masters have learned this truth the hard way. And they will have chelas who stay with them until the final analysis of their problem. Eventually we all come to the fork of the spiritual road in our desire to reach heaven. At this point the chela must accept the way of ECKANKAR, or fall back into his old pattern of beliefs.

Many do this regardless of whether or not they have had the initiation, which is why I insist on chelas having at least two years of study in ECK before being initiated. So many Indian gurus give the initiation first to accept the chela, then they lose him to another. The chela does not take his initiation seriously, and the guru has a hard time holding him.

This should never be. But ECK is a subtle path, and until one realizes this he is not going to advance very far. For example, a woman requested a healing, via the mails, and sent along ten dollars as a donation. Later, she demanded the donation be returned because, according to her, a prayer to one of the Christian saints had been answered and the affliction healed before the letter left her house.

The subtleness of the ECK is that It worked before she had written her letter, while the petition was still in her mind. But in order to confirm her desires for healing she had also requested the saint to give help. The ECK used the lady's consciousness and resolved the condition at once. The petition to the saint was only in her mind.

The chela's strange desire to get something out of the Divine source is best exemplified in a famous historical occurrence. The British defeated the French at Quebec in 1759, giving the English colonies along the Atlantic seaboard freedom from the French and Indians. Strangely, the English won an empire at the treaty table several years later, in Paris, but lost their colonies in America by doing so.

This is also true of the chela, for when he believes that the Master has given him freedom, and then he is asked to assume some of the burdens that must be carried for the works of ECK in this world, the chela will walk away. No one wants to help carry the burden. Naturally, every Master knows this and puts little trust in the human consciousness of man. When man reverts into that primitive state of mind, he lives in fear and doubt. It is hard for anyone to lift himself out of this human consciousness.

Vajra Manjushri, a great ECK Master, learned this during his lifetime in Persia centuries ago. Approximately 700 B.C. he tried to teach ECKANKAR openly to the Persians, but they were too steeped in their own Mithraism under Hakhamanish the First. Manjushri tried to establish ECKANKAR as the true religion but suffered arrest by the King, a mock trial, and death by soldiers who fired arrows into his body as he was stretched out on a rude block of wood that looked like a large "E."

He was the living ECK Master of his time. Those few who had been his followers buried him in a cave with the permission of the King's Guard. The next morning, upon entering the cavern, the followers found the body gone and immediately fell into an argument saying that someone had stolen the body while they slept. Each accused the other.

Suddenly a voice halted the quarrel. "My sons, why do you fight among one another over a piece of clay? I have not left you neither will you nor the world be without me!"

Vajra Manjushri stood before them clothed in a shimmering white robe that all but blinded them. He taught them for twenty-five days and appointed Matax Roraka, the greatest doubter of his little band of followers, to inherit the mantle of spiritual leadership and become the Mahanta. Then he ascended into the spiritual worlds to take his place among the immortal Adepts of the ancient Order of Vairagi.

The chronicle of the ECK Masters in this world is awe-inspiring and beyond comprehension of the human mind. The old records of the Kadath Inscriptions in the Katsupari Monastery show the history of the living ECK Masters throughout the universes. This includes, of course, those who have served on other planets and constellations.

We shall take up the records of these marvelous Adepts in another chapter. However, I point out here that they have been behind major events in the history of mankind and the great changes that have come about in the spiritual and material universes. The ECK Masters are the agents of God, and each who serves in this world is considered the Godman over all the other Masters, regardless of what their position has been in the past or present. He is the direct agent of God in this world and therefore all worlds.

The universes are the vineyard of the living ECK Master and he will colonize all in the name of the SUGMAD. He will place those Souls who have passed beyond on the proper plane and in their proper places as earned out of this life. He will take each chela past the Angel of Death to where he is supposed to be. His loved ones can be brought to him wherever he might be, because he has earned the right. But this is provided there is a distinctive bond between the two Souls. Unless this deep desire exists between those Souls who have lived together on earth, and unless their karma has been

159

eliminated, they cannot be together again in the other worlds. But the real chela is able and powerful enough with the elimination of his karma to pull his mate upward into the higher worlds, after their physical deaths.

All will eventually leave this world anyway because of the terrible disaster that is coming during the middle part of the twenty-first century. The earth's structure, weakened by atomic testing, will break up into earthquakes that will sink most of this continent, much of Japan, the coast of Asia and Africa, and some of Europe, also. This means that whoever is in the areas named will likely meet their own doom. But now the ECK Masters are trying to get people out fast so that they will never have to return again in a physical embodiment.

We have several million years more, as said previously, before the whole world is burned as promised by the ancients. This is the destruction of the lower worlds, and by that time those who are to help in the works of ECK will be taken care of in the worlds of God.

One will meet various states of consciousness in ECKANKAR among the chelas. No two chelas will give the same answer to a single question when asked personally.

For example, when asked the question, "What is your goal in life?" The typical answer is: "To help others." In the absence of true knowledge the answer is likely to be the same everywhere. Few realize this is a negative answer, and would be surprised if told so.

The chelas of ECK should not be interested, in a manner of speaking, in helping their fellow men. What they should be absorbed in is the attainment of God-Realization. If they are more interested in this than anything else in their lives, it is then likely that the help a fellow man needs will be given.

The desire to help one's fellow man is a negative ambition held only by those who are in the lower state of spiritual development. This is the better virtue of human consciousness, found in social reformers, warriors, teachers of school children, politicians and public servants, while there is noth-

160

ing wrong with this ambition it is, nevertheless, one of the lower states and no chela is going to consider this as his goal in life.

What the chela is really interested in doing is to serve God as a channel for the divine ECK power. When he is interested in serving people, then he has only realized his identity in the human state of consciousness. He has realized who he is and what his relationship is in the world with his fellow man. This is a very common state in which we find those like Albert Schweitzer, Sigmund Freud, Maude Adams, Winston Churchill, Thomas Jefferson, Shakespeare, Pasteur and Rousseau. No criticism is intended towards what these persons and many others have done for mankind, for it is a very marvelous task to help relieve the suffering of a brother in this world. But it is still in the physical and on the human level. We should be more interested in working for the state of God-Realization which prepares us to work for the universal cause.

The world today is filled with darkness, pain and grief. Every individual must seek the path for himself and walk on it himself. The spiritual darkness which broods over the world has created a sickness and the whole of humanity is blind and deaf to the truth of God. Few are interested, nor do they know why they stumble and fall in their spiritual plight of trying to find the path to God. Most persons are suffering from physical illness, heart-sickness, and are worn and weary from their spiritual search.

The masses of people are groping along an uneasy way towards some unknown destiny. None have freedom; they are not even masters of their own bodies, and generally are driven slaves to a job, family responsibilities, and social duties. The unrest which is sweeping the world is understandable. Even despite the drug problem, alcoholism, religious fads and psychic disruptions, sickness of the mind is growing into enormous proportions. But why?

Man has nothing to cling to as an inner support. He has long been a victim of the metaphysicians and clergy who claim they have the remedy for the disease of restlessness.

161

Buddha never found it. Christ made an unnecessary sacrifice for His people, and other saviours and adepts have tried to bring about the cure. Their search has just not gone far enough, despite the fact that at least three thousand different forms of religions have appeared since the beginning of history.

In the absence of knowledge the masses have turned to religion, which is better than no light at all. Usually, when the founders of religion—who are men of spiritual insight—penetrate some subtle plane and try to get established there, they have had to leave this world. Their work is left to immature followers who are generally confused by it. Seldom does any disciple become a real spiritual master, which means they cannot give truth as reality. This is why the world is never without an ECK Master. They do not trust the spiritual works of ECKANKAR to their disciples.

While we do not condemn religions, it is best to say that none go as far as the true chela desires. Few in churches have ever been able to reach Self-Realization, let alone God-Realization. And we must remember that the ultimate end of all spiritual works is the realization of God, not merely feeling and thinking about It. There is, beyond all books, creeds, and vanities of the world, the realization of God. A man might believe in the church, have knowledge of the sacred books of this world, and might be baptized a hundred times into a hundred different creeds, but he will not have achieved spiritual unfoldment because he has not learned anything about God.

Realization of God is not gained by metaphysical speculation, nor by feeling, logic, or any mental device. It is gained when one practices the spiritual exercises of ECKANKAR. One cannot get Self-Realization, until he is able to do Soul Travel.

We will therefore compare the various religions with what ECK is offering the true seeker of God in the world today. There are at least a dozen major orthodox religions throughout the world. In the past there were many more, such as the ancient religions of Animism, Polytheism and Anthropomorphism; of Egypt; Sumerian, Assyrian, Babylonian and Hittite religions; the Mystery religions of Greece; Mithraism; Manichaeism; Mazdaism; Shamanism; the Norse religions and those of the North American Indians.

Close study will show that present day religions are an adaptation of the ancient religions just named. The modern faiths are Hinduism, Buddhism, Confucianism, Taoism, Islamism, Judaism, Zoroastrianism, Sikhism, Theosophy, Christian Science, Shintoism, Spiritualism, Ba'hai and Christianity. The leaders in numbers of followers are: Hinduism, Buddhism and Christianity, all three of whose members run into the millions.

All religions, philosophies and sacred doctrines are the offspring of ECKANKAR. Nothing could exist without the essence of the ECK which flows out of the heart of the SUGMAD and builds embodiments, sustains life, and creates Souls. All entities from the mineral consciousness to those serving as co-workers for God are sustained by the ECK. Each of the orthodox religions had a founder who has come and gone in his physical body. It may be noted that, as in Christianity, Christ is called the "Light of the World," so in the Orient Buddha is given the title "Light of Asia." Followers of other faiths in turn gave their leaders titles similar to this, but the living ECK Master, the Mahanta, is known as the "Light of the Universes."

Unless a religion has a living Master, one who is in the flesh and able to perform in the spiritual body also, that faith is dead. This is fundamental to all religions. It means that every spiritual Master who has walked this Earth and taught, was giving out knowledge relative to his own times. This is true of Zoroaster, Buddha, Christ and other spiritual giants. But it is not true of the living ECK Masters.

The living ECK Master is timeless in the Atma Sarup. He is the Alpha and Omega, immaculately conceived, raised in the physical form within this world according to the laws of nature, until he eventually dies in this form. He may be kept on Earth for a long period of time for particular missions, or he may pass on after only a short time on this planet, to serve in the spiritual worlds. Some live a normal life span, while a few meet with violent deaths. Their mission in life determines just how long they will be in the physical embodiment.

Every ECK Master must go through the initiation, or rites of accepting the Rod of ECK power, when he accepts the spiritual mantle. He must, in a sense, publicly state before all the spiritual Masters of the past, the Nine Unknown ECK Masters, and his own Master, that he will fulfill the duties of the Mahanta while wearing the title. He cannot in any way escape his responsibilities once the Rod of ECK power is accepted.

It is during this ritual that the ECK descends and enters into the new Master, giving him the power of the Word of God. He becomes the actual manifestation of God through this power, which he retains throughout his life here on Earth and throughout the universes. There is no spiritual line of Masters so ancient and so all-powerful as the ECK Masters. When living in the physical body as the mentor of humanity they are saviours of the human race.

Be that as it may, the modern religions and their works are:

1. Hinduism: This is the religion of the vast majority of the people of India. It is the supreme example of polytheism. Its principal Gods are Brahma, Shiva and Vishnu. Its holy books are the Vedas and the Upanishads. Its main feature is Cosmic Consciousness, which is an enlightenment of the intellectual senses taking one only to the mental realm, which is the region of the Brahma. Offshoots include yoga followers, Vedantists, and others.

The followers of Hinduism cannot go beyond the mental plane with their system of meditation. Many yogis hardly reach the pure astral world.

2. Buddhism: Buddhism is based upon the teachings of Nepalese Prince Siddhartha Gautama, who became the Buddha. He lived about 500 years B.C. There are about 200

million Buddhists in the Orient, without counting those outside Asia. It includes the Mahayana branch in the northern part of Asia, which stresses salvation and contemplation, and Hinayana, which preserves the monastic teachings of the early believers. This branch is prominent in southeast Asia. Zen is another part of Buddhism, stressing introspection, self-examination and gentleness. Lamaism of Tibet is a combination of Buddhism and the primitive beliefs of that country.

Buddhism places its emphasis upon the mental part of man. It originally split from Hinduism, borrowing from it Satori, or enlightenment, and Cosmic Consciousness. Both of these are mental plane phenomena. Followers of this religion seldom get that far.

3. **Confucianism:** This is really not a religion, although it is called one. It was founded by Confucius, or Klung Fu-tse, and is based upon a system of ethical rules for the proper management of human affairs. Confucius, who lived in the sixth century B.C., was a government official. His works do not have the spiritual value that they are believed to have. There are no significant lines in them concerning Soul Travel or any path to God.

4. **Taoism:** Taoism arose in China about the sixth century, B.C. It is based upon the Tao-Te-Ching, by the legendary philosopher Lao-Tze. Tao means path, and the basis of early Taoism was that the affairs of man should take the path of Nature. The religion stresses quietism, contemplation, and the elimination of striving and strong passions. It provided the foundation for many secret societies in China. But nowhere does it stress the factor of Soul Travel, or reaching the heart of God. It is very vague about God and the Divine aspects.

5. **Islamism:** The word Islam means "submission to or being at peace with God." This religion was founded by Mohammed, who was born in Mecca during the sixth century, A.D. The moral precepts of the Moslems extend to all areas of secular and civil life. The four duties for the follower of

Islam are: recitation of prayers, observance of Ramadan, self-examination, and a period of fasting one month long. One must make a pilgrimage to Mecca if possible, and of necessity must give alms and pray five times daily facing in the direction of Mecca.

There is not much here to bring one into the spiritual realm, only faith and the belief that after death one will be taken care of in a heavenly paradise. Nothing about God-Realization is found in the Koran, the sacred scriptures of the Moslem faith.

6. Judaism: This is the oldest monotheistic religion in the world. Its followers worship a God called Jehovah, who is the Supreme Being for all orthodox Jews. The sacred book of Judaism is the Old Testament—particularly the Torah, or the first five books—and the Talmud, a collection of later teachings and interpretation. Their creed is a summary of the Jews' experiences over 3,500 years.

The mystical teaching of the Jews is the Cabbalah. It is a doctrine containing mystical interpretations of Jewish scripture, and metaphysical speculations concerning their Supreme Deity, man, and spiritual beings. It is divided into the practical and theoretical. The practical is occupied with instruction in talismans and amulets. The theoretical is divided into the dogmatic and literal. But there is nothing within the whole of Judaism that shows a living Master, nor the sound current of ECK. Unless a religion has as its basis light and sound, then it is not built upon a solid spiritual foundation.

7. Zoroastrianism: This religion was developed in eastern Persia by Zarathustra, who became known as Zoroaster. Its chief sacred text is the Zend Avesta, which is a collection of the writings of Zoroaster. Its modern representatives are the Parsees of India, sometimes called the Fire Worshippers, because they look upon fire and the sun as symbolic of the Supreme One. This Supreme Lord is called Ahura-Mazda or Ormuzd. The main theme of their writings is the ethical

and dualistic struggle between good and evil, or light and darkness.

It was formed about six hundred years before the transition from ancient to modern times, when Zoroaster, who was an Aryan, brought to the peoples of Persia and the mid-East a religion that was to change them from a primitive to a cultured environment. Out of this came the famed Order of the Magi, the wise men of the East. Again, we do not find the ECK sound current in these teachings, and this must always be the basis for pure works. Zoroastrianism is a dualistic religion, while truly spiritual workings do not recognize evil or any dichotomy in the attributes of the SUGMAD.

8. Sikhism: The Sikh religion is another minor one, limited largely to Punjab, in India. It was founded by Guru Nanak during the fifteenth century. A contemporary of Kabir, famed Hindu mystic, he came in contact with ECKANKAR and taught what he knew of it. His deviation from ECK was that he thought no more living gurus would follow the last of his nine successors, and from that time on the Granth Sahib, the sacred book of the Sikhs, became the Guru to all, as the Bible is to the Christians. Guru Nanak was the only living saint produced in this religion. He gained a high state of consciousness, but none were able to follow him. Yet he did not teach the light and sound as it is taught in ECK.

9. Theosophy: This is a system of religious, philosophical teachings, coupled with the personal experiences of Madame Blavatsky. Together it sums up some of the eastern wisdoms. It is based almost entirely upon the Vedas and the Upanishads of Hinduism. It does not deal at all with ECKANKAR, for its founder does not appear to have known anything about it whatsoever. The sound current has been completely side-tracked.

Madame Blavatsky was an authority on the Great White Brotherhood, which makes its headquarters in the Himalayas.

They are only a part of the spiritual hierarchy on this plane, charged by the ECK Masters to keep a vigilant eye on the world's evolution.

10. Christian Science: This is a better known branch of orthodox Christianity. It is a protest against the general unhappiness with modern Christianity. Mary Baker Eddy, founder of Christian Science, believed that all sin, pain, sickness, and evils of every sort were only mental illusions. Her main textbook, Keys to Science and Health, is a doctrine of metaphysical postulates stating that healings are possible in every department of one's life, especially for diseases and ill health. It does not go much further than this.

11. Shintoism: The origin of this ancient religion is lost in antiquity. Until the fifth century, A.D., the Shinto tradition was oral, and no written documents existed. In Japan, however, we find a modified form of Shintoism surviving for 53 million believers.

It is a set of rituals and customs involving pilgrimages, festivals, and the worship of several Gods. It grew from a primitive nature worship, was later influenced by Buddhism, and eventually became the state religion of Japan.

Shintoism has no ethical or moral system except emphasis on ceremonial life and bodily cleanliness. A sun goddess was long known as the chief deity, the ruler of heaven, until roughly the seventh century, when the Emperor became the immortal head. From this a state form of Shintoism was organized to glorify the militaristic philosophy of the government. After World War II, this was disbanded and the present Emperor disavowed his divinity.

12. Jainism: This is another religion of India of antiquity. The last of its great teachers — called Tirthankaras — was Mahavira, who lived during the sixth century, B.C. Jainism embraces many philosophical concepts of the Indian religions. Its main principle is non-violence toward all living things. This means neither insects, other creatures, nor people, can be killed, and no harm can come to nature. According

to Jainism, the world is eternal and subject to six stages of good and evil, but we in ECKANKAR know that it is part of God's nature to periodically destroy and recreate the lower planes during the great yugas. It has no living master, nor does it seem to have any part of the light and sound in its sacred writings, the Shvetambara. Most of Jainism is concerned with karma and its basic principle, "harm no one."

13. Spiritualism: This movement has grown since World War II due to global crises. Its central theme is communication, through a medium, between this world and the spirit-physical worlds. This communication takes place on the psychic level. True spiritualism does not believe in reincarnation. It was started in New York by the Fox sisters during the middle part of the past century, and grew largely through the expository efforts of Andrew Jackson Davis. The departed Soul goes to what the Spiritualistic philosophy calls "The Summerland." It is a region between the earth spheres and the first region of the pure astral plane.

14. Christianity: This is the best known religion in the Western world. It was created by St. Paul, who sold the teachings of Jesus Christ to the world according to his conception of what Christianity might be. He was not a follower of Christ in the beginning, nor did he ever know Him. As with many other religions, the words of the original leader have not been given to the world in their true light. Christianity has given a great deal of satisfaction to millions of followers, yet it has had its failures like all religious groups. Its book is the New Testament, containing the Gospels, which are based on the teachings of love and right action. The living leader, Jesus Christ, placed His spiritual heritage in the hands of Simon Peter, but after his departure the line of spiritual masters passed away.

Christianity speaks somewhat of the sound and light but these references are vague. The Word, which is the physical manifestation of the ECK, is stated forthrightly in the Gospel of John, but it can hardly be found anywhere else.

Religions are formal teachings belonging to the growth of certain races during corresponding periods of human thought and evolution. Each religion served its own purpose in its own day and time. But each must give way to something more complete as humanity advances. Throughout human history the basic reason for any and all religions has been an effort to know and understand God, but only a few have succeeded.

Man has yet to learn that his desires bind him to the object of his desires. ECK says the chela must have complete detachment from every worldly object, to avoid bondage to the things of the material worlds. Anyone who looks for rewards in this world will become a slave to such rewards. He gets most by giving most· by receiving one impoverishes himself.

The ECK is the way to God. This is our basic teaching. Whenever men pursue creeds, priests and organization, they will find a religion of some sort but never the Way to enter the Kingdom of God as stated by the great ECK Masters.

So many have the misconception that moral goodness is a requirement for spiritual salvation. This is not true. Moral goodness comes only from spiritual salvation.

The main teaching of ECKANKAR is that if the chela faithfully practices the spiritual exercises, he will enter the Kingdom of Heaven while still living in the human body. This is the fundamental difference between ECK and all other religions. Also, ECK alone offers a living leader, for as spiritual law clearly states: "The chela in a human body must have a Master in the human body."

Any system that does not make the ECK the central theme of its spiritual exercises can never withstand the downward drag of mind and matter. Without the ECK in his life the chela cannot journey very far on the road to the Kingdom of God. Every advanced chela will attest that there is no spiritual freedom for anyone until he learns to follow the living ECK Master. The Mahanta is a spiritual liberator. He does not work through a spiritualist medium, nor is he the world builder so many religions make of their leaders. The living Master is here to take a personal interest in all who desire to find the way home to God via the ECK path.

The cardinal principle of spiritual law is the necessity of the living ECK Master, appointed by the SUGMAD to represent the Kingdom of God in this world. This means that only one who is still in the physical body can be appointed. It is a fixed law that only the Mahanta in his human body can act as the Master for those still in their human bodies. Only man can teach man, and only man can initiate man. The departed ECK Master will take care of all whom he has initiated, but he does not accept any new disciples. This is not a limitation of his powers; it is the chela himself who is so limited he cannot receive instructions and initiation from an invisible Master. If the departed Master could take care of new disciples, there would be no need for Masters at all on the physical level. The SUGMAD could do all the work without assistance. But man cannot be taught by any other agency than another in a physical embodiment.

A humanly embodied Master is necessary because of the limitations of the chela. That difficulty cannot be surmounted in any possible way except for God to manifest Itself in human form.

The next fundamental point of ECK is the ECK Life Stream. The living ECK Masters have emphasized this sound current as the cornerstone of Soul Travel. It is nothing more than the Supreme Deity projecting Itself to all planes in all universes in a constant wave of harmonious and musical vibrations, through which flows the life-giving and creative, all-comprehensive Power of God.

Complete liberation and spiritual freedom gained while living in the physical body is the third ECK principle. It is not necessary to wait until after death to attain freedom, as most religions tell us. This is the failure of those religions and the triumph of ECKANKAR. This freedom is achieved by the spiritual exercises of ECK, and if they are not begun during this life spiritual liberation cannot be accomplished after death.

The fourth precept is that one who cannot initiate and lead the chela into the inner worlds, is not a living ECK Master. Initiation is essential for no one can travel very far without it, and the living ECK Master is the only one who can give it.

The great links in the chain of spiritual salvation are: the living ECK Master, the ECK Life Stream, and spiritual liberation. This is the way to God via the path of ECK.

Chapter Eleven

THE LOWER VERSUS HIGHER POWERS

The raging conflict between the Kal power and the ECK power is eternal in the psychic worlds, which are all those below the fifth plane. Few chelas ever recognize this battle but blame it upon something materialistic or some person. This is a common practice of the ignorant.

The battle is the fight between good and evil. Kal is, according to Christian terminology, Satan, or the Devil, while ECK is the true essence of the Lord of all Lords. It is not the actual Godhead, but a manifestation of God. It is the Holy Ghost, the Comforter, the Divine Spirit which flows from the throne of the SUGMAD.

The Kal is the Universal Mind Power, the essence of a being called Kal Niranjan, the King of the lower worlds. The SUGMAD created the Kal for a purpose. He is the King of Negative Power, established on his throne to create obstacles and so test Soul, that it may temper and perfect Itself in Its rounds on the Wheel of the Eighty-Four. In other words, the lower worlds were created as a training ground for Soul to gather knowledge and eventually graduate to the higher worlds so it can serve as a co-worker with God.

Unless Soul takes the path of ECK there is no salvation or liberation for It. All other paths lead only to the top of the three worlds—the physical, astral and mental—where sits the throne of Kal Niranjan. There the individual ends up serving this entity instead of God. The Kal will establish traps, barriers, and false signs, leading not to God but to the top of the mind world, where he himself dwells.

The ways of the ECK are subtle and forceful. It does not enforce spiritual laws like a civilian police force. It does not bind Souls to Itself with a covenant of words, nor does It reach out and shove a person onto the path to God. Instead the chela will find that It shows the way to God; it nudges him and tries to make him recognize right guidance.

Kal does not work in the same manner. It overpowers the individual with laws and punishments. It degenerates the individual's noble ideals into a futility of purpose. It uses public opinion, traditional beliefs, attachments to desires, and glittering promises of gold and false happiness. It whispers sweet dreams into the chela's ears and promises much in order to keep him off the path of ECK.

This is the test, the trial and the ritual of fire that the chela undergoes. The greatest good that he can achieve is to serve the living ECK Master, and to die in the cause of ECK is the sublime end of all things.

This service generates power to work off all the chela's worldly karma, no matter if he has served ECK for one day or a thousand years. He is taken by the Master into the heavenly worlds and placed there because he has earned his place. He shall be the recipient of all heavenly delights that come with living in the higher planes.

It matters not whether or not he is able to do actual Soul Travel, for service and self-surrender are the basis for all rewards in heaven. The very fact that he makes an effort at doing the spiritual exercises creates spiritual merit and gives him longevity, love, and a permanent residence in heaven with loved ones. Therefore, all ECK chelas practice the Hakku-Ichiu-ECK, which is "bringing the eight corners of the world under the roof of ECK."

The chela does not die for the materialistic things of this world, but for the ideal of the SUGMAD. The greatness of the ECK chela is not based upon his intellectual powers but is measured by his willingness to devote all his faculties to the service of the living ECK Master. The true chela is willing to give up everything in his life to serve the cause of the Master and ECK.

ECK has a way of enforcing Its decisions, but few ever recognize this. Unless the chela has some means of looking to this subtle guidance which the ECK gives him, he finds failure in his life. ECK does not use the power of civil law and public opinion, which are aspects of the negative force. This force, in the absence of resistance, takes over the chela and pushes him toward the Kal. The chela must bind himself to the ECK Master with deeds and actions, not with the covenant of words that will rapidly degenerate into a noble futility.

Until he learns to do everything for the living ECK Master, and learns that every deed, thought and interest in life is done in the name of the Master, he is bound to be a wanderer. If he leaves the path of ECK to go to what his senses tell him is better, or what he believes is greater, then he is deluding himself and will dwell forever in the lower astral worlds. He will dwell there until these aspects of the negative are given up; then the Master will lift him out, placing him upon one of the higher planes.

Anyone who puts faith in anything other than the living ECK Master has no support for his life. Unless the chela turns his inner life over to the Master, not much can be done for him. This means that few chelas will succeed because they do not know how to surrender to him, nor do they wish to do this. Too many things stand in their way, the greatest of which is pride.

Pride, which is an aspect of vanity, is the worst perversion of the mental faculties that one can have. This is especially true in the spiritual works. When one has spiritual pride he is much further down the spiritual ladder than most chelas. He is in a stalemate and cannot break out of it until he recognizes this deadly perversion of his mind and becomes humble in the presence of the living ECK Master.

One of the most common manifestations of vanity is pretended humility. It makes one swell with pride over some trifling victory or virtue. Self-righteousness is one of the most prevalent and most malignant mental diseases that can affect the chela. It is well known to those who are on the path that egotism is the last to surrender. Its method is to distort the view point, to present everything out of proportion and make itself the center of the world. It destroys all sense of humor, for if they had it they would not be vain.

The chief function of vanity is to block the path of truth. It is one of the main weapons of the Kal. It completely deceives its victims, making them self-satisfied and content to live in the lower worlds when they should be seeking to get out of the morass of negativity.

The methods of the Kal can be very subtle. For example, saints of the negative worlds say they have set out to destroy the evildoers. In the Bhagavad Gita Krishna said,"I come forth for the protection of the good, for the destruction of the evildoers, for the sake of firmly establishing righteousness. I am born from age to age."

Compare the two missions. Krishna comes, as the reincarnation of Vishnu, to improve the world. But the ECK Master comes to deliver men from the bondage of this world, not to improve it. It is the duty of the Kal, of whom Krishna was an incarnation, to keep this world at least a livable place. Bad at its best, it must not be allowed to get worse for those living within it. Thus, we can compare the two missions—one of the negative power and the other of the positive—as the difference between living in a prison and living free. While in prison, the inmates must have things that will make their lives more tolerable. So those inclined toward charity offer them something to make their lives in prison more bearable. But eventually one with power to release the prisoner arrives, freeing him and saying that now he may live without restrictions.

The agents of the negative power seek only to hold Soul in this world. They make Its life livable while here but do nothing to set It free. But the ECK Master, who is the liberator, is here to give each Soul Its freedom and a lift into the heavenly worlds.

Krishna says that he comes to destroy the evildoer. This is entirely different from what the ECK Master does. He has no intention of destruction, but comes to redeem and liberate the evildoer so he can become a higher chela and eventually return to his heavenly home. Thus the ECK Master gathers the desolate, hungry and weary Souls, and by the aid of the

ECK, the sound current, delivers them from the bondage of this world. This is the essential difference between the works of the ECK Master and the agents of the Kal.

Further examination of the difference between the two powers shows that the negative uses various words for their degrees of uplifting Soul to the higher levels. For example, the secret method of meditation for the yogis is the ancient custom of repeating the sacred word OM. This is about all the ancient or modern yogis have ever employed in their meditation.

If the student of yoga undertakes to practice this method of meditation he will surely get some results, but not enough to escape the evils of the psychic worlds. He will gain some degree of mental poise and he will find an increase in the joy of living, but this is just about all he will receive. He can become a better and more useful citizen to this world, and dwell in some quiet corner of the astral world, but he must return to the regions of matter for rebirth. Even though this is a better position than many, it is still not the ultimate place that the chela wants.

Few, if any, yogis go beyond the Brahm Lok. But the ECK chela can go far beyond this into the Soul world, and eventually into the God worlds. This is a very important distinction to keep in mind. One must beware, however, of the dangers that beset the path of the chela, for he may be misled into believing that he has actually attained the highest on the spiritual path; that he has reached the regions of immortality, and is beyond the reach of the Wheel of the Eighty-Four.

Many have believed this only to later discover their mistake; the Kal has taken advantage of their ignorance and established a curtain of illusion to blind them. Some have not discovered this error yet, and it could be many incarnations before they learn of their fatal mistake.

No Soul, by the use of OM and the methods of the yogis, ever goes any further than the mind plane. Neither will it escape the mind and matter regions until it takes up the path of ECK. Millions of Souls will and can rise to the beautiful worlds of the astral and causal planes, where the light is glorious and they experience long periods of rest and enjoyment of earned karma. But this is all a part of the clever scheme of Kal.

Although the Bhagavad Gita says that the yogi will have no more rebirths or deaths, it is not true. It leads to delusion, for the Kal has cunningly arranged a system leading the yogi to believe he has found the way, while being held a prisoner by Kal. This is true not only of the yogi but of most of the great religious and metaphysical systems that try to prove they have the ultimate way.

The paths that these two lower systems offer are better than no path, but ECK is the only way. The follower of either the metaphysical or the religious path can go just so far. Each chela who has gone to the higher planes knows that the higher he goes, the more difficult the path becomes without the ECK Master. Soon, the stage is reached where it is impossible to go any further without the presence and help of the living ECK Master.

Exposure to mysticism is most intriguing but few are ready to enter into this spiritual field. Those who are not ready are opened to dangerous psychic forces which bring them into the areas of deep neurosis, paranoia and schizophrenia. They become a detriment to society, yet they are praised by the news media and those in responsible and influential positions. Out of this has come psychedelic and zodiacal paraphernalia. These are astral influences, some of the many aspects of Kal, and not good for the individual or for mankind. They only hold back man's spiritual progress.

The chela must never think of the SUGMAD as a gigantic Deity sitting on a throne somewhere in space, manipulating people by strings, or as that image Michelangelo established with his famous murals of the Supreme Being. Instead, the chela must be aware of the SUGMAD as that Divine Source which has ITS power invested in the living ECK Master.

178

I say here, "Be aware." This is the difference between the mental and the true spiritual worlds. Thus awareness is consciousness, and until one comes to recognize it within him self, he will never gain much spiritual unfoldment. Con sciousness is beyond the worlds of thought. It is the foundation of ECK, and the whole of ECK teachings. It is the explanation for the difference between the mental and Soul plane. It is the hardest dividing line to cross.

The problem of every chela who walks the path of ECK is separating these two states. His first encounter with life is the separation of the physical from the emotional and the emotional from thought. The last state is to separate thought from consciousness. This is almost impossible for many people, and the very reason why they fail in the spiritual exercises of ECK.

The secret of entering into the consciousness state is detaching one's self from the outer, or sense world, and withdrawing one's attention from all sensory objects. Then the chela begins to concentrate his attention on something inside. So far this is the general method of all systems. But the secret is that the mental world—which consists of the tools of thought—and every plane below it, comprise the negative worlds. They lie within the realm of Kal Niranjan, whose responsibility it is to keep each Soul occupied so that It is too busy with the wonders of the negative world to desire anything better. Naturally, most of the ambitions and desires that one has for God are really in the negative sense. If the chela has a desire and ambition for God-Realization, then he is seeking the wrong way. The words, "desire" and "ambition" explain clearly that he is using negative tools to seek a positive result. When he detaches himself from these aspects, he begins to gain results in the spiritual senses. He crosses the boundary between conciousness and thought.

The chela will eventually realize that the mind is a useful servant but a bad master. It is only the chela of the living ECK Master who is given every protection against the deceptions of the mind powers. It is only the chela of the ECK Master who can separate the difference between the Universal

179

Mind Power and the ECK, as he begins to enter those subtle regions of the mind world. He cannot do without the guidance of the living ECK Master in these dangerous zones.

I have pointed this out strongly in the spiritual works of ECK, especially in the brochure, "The Dangers of the Psychic World for Truth Seekers." The mind will play a thousand tricks upon the chela. It is unreliable and habitually beset by its own thought creations, harrassed by its own desires and dominated by its own passions. The ECK Master offers a perfect safeguard against the disasters the chela encounters when following the dictates of the mental powers.

The world is a stage for the intellect. It is one of the negative power's fields of operation, and known as the play of the mind. But there is a vast field of consciousness far above and beyond the play of the mind where the perfected chela may enter.

Consciousness is the ultimate reality of all things—a presence we are aware of but cannot explain. It is an unmanifested force, a presence which has no being, and does not perform any function. This alone makes it different from the audible life current, the ECK. Only because of Its presence are all life forms conscious.

There are various degrees of consciousness, although the knowingness of it is the same. For example, the consciousness of a stone is certainly different from the consciousness of man. So the further into the inner worlds that Soul travels, the greater is the awareness of this consciousness developed. This is what I speak about so often when discussing the higher conciousness and the lower consciousness. It consists in recognizing its existence in each of us and all around us. The religious thinkers mix this with intellect.

Others interpret this as God, but it is not. Some think that is the Divine Spirit, but again it is not. It is the force that we call love; that which binds life and all things together in an adhesiveness that cannot be broken. Because of this many religions are founded on love, though not as a conscious fact. It has been built up on the subconscious level, for most people—including thinkers and theologians—think of love in a sentimental fashion. This attitude has created more wars and upheavals in the human race than anything else in the religious field. In trying to get others to love us we take up the sword, believing that it is right. Torquemada, the Spanish Grand Inquisitor during the fifteenth century, believed he was right in creating terror and death for the enemies of the Catholic Church. But he was deceived by the negative power into thinking that his torture of his fellow man was for good and justice.

Spiritual law states that: "No man can discover the living ECK Master until certain inner preparations have been made." And: "No man can receive the initiation into ECK-ANKAR until he has had the proper spiritual unfoldment. It is the living ECK Master who is aware of this, and the judge as to whether the chela shall be initiated."

This is the secret of the relationship between the living ECK Master and the chela, unraveling the mystery surrounding initiation. The Master never charges for initiation because it is against the spiritual law. When a chela has unfolded spiritually to the point of initiation then he is able to receive it, for he has worked out enough karma to take care of the payment of the debt.

Soul is the real man, the Atma, the Purusha, or the creative spark in the individual. It is the glimmer of light from Heaven, a drop of the Ocean of Being. It is in Soul that all consciousness resides, and all power. Everything below Soul, even the mind itself, is unconscious, automatic, and mechanical in action. Everything in existence is dependent entirely upon the ECK for its life, and since consciousness resides in Soul, then It, of Itself, is the channel for God.

Everything outside of Soul lies in the world of Karma. Each must pay his own debts. "No one else can ever pay the debt of another," said Rebazar Tarzs when asked by someone to take the karmic burden of a sick son. "I can give him help but he must, of his own self, pay his debts to God."

The Master will sometimes take upon himself the karmic debt of another, if he believes that it will help, but not often. He wants every chela to stand on his own feet. He

181

watches over the chela during his struggles against the Kal forces, and protects him whenever allowed. The chela has only to look for the living ECK Master to open the way for him. The Master will help him to awaken all his sleeping faculties and liberate his latent powers. By doing this he will come into conscious contact with the entire system of worlds, both physical and spiritual; filling all space, beyond all time. The exact process by which this can be accomplished is revealed by the ECK Master to each chela who follows him.

Man himself is so constructed that he is able to consciously communicate with the worlds within worlds, and if he is properly guided he can do Soul Travel. All he needs is the system, and this is the path of ECK. Each and every man, when properly trained, is able to detach himself from the physical body, while still living in it, and travel to all parts of the spiritual universe.

When spiritual power comes to the chela, consciousness will also come to him. The chela must recognize this. He must learn to beware of the price he pays when he sells his will to powers other than the living ECK Master. If the chela does nothing else but give himself up entirely to the living ECK Master, he has gained eternity. But should he give himself up to the will of the negative power, he has gained nothing.

The chela's greatest problem in the Kal worlds is his struggle with the senses. The senses of the physical self create desire, which is the trap of the lower worlds. The senses overwhelm the mind, when strong enough, and the mind then enslaves Soul. Following desire, the mind goes on creating karma and entangling itself in the web of karmic patterns.

The ECK is God ITSELF in expression. The fact that it is audible is extremely important, and this idea must be conveyed, if possible, to all chelas as the sum of all teachings. This is why ECK is the original source, the mainstream of all religious teachings. This is how we know that life springs from ECKANKAR, or what we know as the SUGMAD.

The spiritual works of ECK are the primitive teachings of God. It, the Word, is the language of God; it is God expressing ITSELF, which is the heart of all spiritual matters. The word Nam means "name" in Sanskrit, therefore, we speak of the SUGMAD in Name or Word. The Word also means what God says and does. It is the Divine Being in action, but we must separate God in action from God as the Divine Consciousness. Thus we call this action the living ECK, or the living Word.

When we speak of the ECK as the living Word, or God in action, we are speaking of the media upon which the God Essence, or Spirit, moves. This is similar to a wave emanating from the Ocean of Love and Mercy. The sound Itself represents all attributes of God, and is the only way that God can manifest ITSELF to the human consciousness. When God manifested ITSELF as the Sat Nam in Sach Khand, the Soul plane of the spiritual worlds, IT became fully personified, embodied, and individualized for the first time, bringing into manifestation all qualities of the SUGMAD.

The initiates of ECK must learn this lesson well about the audible life current. Unless they do, none will receive the third initiation. Any chela who refuses to attain the state of self-surrender to the living ECK Master can not expect to go beyond the second level of initiation.

Unless the chela gives up his questions, vanity, lust, anger, and attachment to the material things of life and greed, he will never have the pleasure of hearing the ECK speak to him. It is only when man hears the ECK that he hears God, for the ECK is the Divine SUGMAD expressing ITSELF in everything that is both audible and visible. This Word, or sound, is the creative energy that gives Soul Its power. By this Sat Nam created the lower worlds, and established Kal Niranjan upon his throne to act as the counteracting Force to perfect each Soul.

This action was similar to the establishment of an educational system for training children to fit into the social order when they mature. Thus did God establish a training system for Souls, so they might fit into the spiritual order when matured. Those within the framework of the spiritual society are co-workers with God. Those who have not yet traveled the path of ECK, nor met the living ECK Master, will have to incarnate over and over on the Wheel of the Eighty-Four until the day arrives when they are spiritually developed enough to meet the Master and begin their journey to the heavenly worlds.

Man is so created and constituted that everything connected with him in the human state of mind has a limited range. His ear can only receive sounds that are within a given range; just so high and no higher, just so low and no lower. Beyond these points he cannot hear existing sounds, because they are out of his range of reception. This is true of all the physical senses. Also, whether or not the individual believes it, it is true of the psychic senses. But it is not true of the senses or faculties of Soul. Once the individual begins to dwell in Soul consciousness, he is capable of knowing and seeing all things. This is why he who is able to do Soul Travel should be able to read the Soul and ECK Vidya records for anyone. Those who are dwelling in the psychic senses can do neither of these, only Akashic readings and astrological charts. The latter is actually a mechanical process.

Therefore the ECK, the audible life stream, should be heard and felt in the innermost consciousness, like the whispering of some mysterious voice throughout all space. The melodies of the Divine ECK are floating through all worlds, including the lower worlds. This life stream is inside ourselves; it is a part of each individual, but this Kingdom must be entered and explored by the Light and the Word of the ECK.

The living ECK Master and many of the chelas pass daily through the Gates of Death, and know the problems connected with this experience. They explore worlds upon worlds beyond those Gates, under the guidance and protection of the Master and in full consciousness, as a direct result of their practice of the spiritual exercises of ECK.

The ECK Master never loses consciousness, and when he returns to his body he has complete memory of every experience he went through during the absence from his physical form. This he shows his own chelas how to do. The chela will, in time, learn to step out of his body at will and in full possession of all his faculties. He will learn, under the guidance of the ECK Master, to know what he is doing and remain in control of the process. However, if a chela does not learn this during his time on earth, it will not go against him. If he gives love, loyalty and service to the living ECK Master, he will work off his karma and earn a high place in the spiritual worlds after death.

When the living ECK Master leaves his body and travels in the other worlds, taking many of his chelas with him, he functions on whatever plane necessary and in the respective body of that plane. He is the Master of all regions and planes. He shows each chela, in the chela's own way, how to discard all bodies and act as a free Soul, anywhere, and unhindered. But always under the direction of the Master.

CHAPTER TWELVE

THE ULTIMATE AWARENESS OF GOD

Those who follow the path of ECK, by reason of their application of the power of the SUGMAD, become possessed of spiritual powers that are not consciously manifested by the average individual.

Such awareness lies in the area of God-Realization. When one reaches this level of consciousness he has these powers, styled "supernatural," or above and beyond the normal powers exercised by the great masses of people. One must look closely at this, though, because of the difference between supernormal and supernatural powers. They are not to be identified with one another.

The supernormal powers are the mind forces, belonging in the area of the Kal power. These are strictly normal powers exercised by those who know how to manipulate the mind forces for their own or others' benefit. Keep this distinction in mind when examining the spiritual works of ECK.

The ECK Masters are well versed in supernatural powers. They never use the lower powers for any need, however, and this is the reason why few return after they have passed their earthly incarnation as the living ECK Master. Each is working at his own respective duty somewhere in the spiritual worlds. If anyone has an affinity for an ECK Master who has passed from this world into the spiritual regions, he should drop it and turn to the present living ECK Master. The departed Masters seldom, if at any time, give the necessary support and help to any chelas except those who were their own during their last respective incarnation on earth.

If any chela of the Mahanta, the living ECK Master, should attempt to send out a request to one of these departed masters in hopes of assistance, he will be disappointed, for rarely will any departed Master respond. The reason for this is that none ever use the lower powers. Should they be called upon to give spiritual assistance, to comply they would have to lower themselves to the level of the chela who made the call. This they do not do.

The chela may receive the teachings from any of them at their respective Temples of Golden Wisdom, where many teach from the Shariyat-Ki-Sugmad. But in this case the chela is lifted up to these planes by the living ECK Master and given over to the Master who is in charge there. The chela cannot go alone, for he is not allowed to enter any Temple of Golden Wisdom unless accompanied by the Mahanta, the living ECK Master.

The ECK always re-embodies Itself in some physical manifestation, in one called the living ECK Master. To study this phase of ECKANKAR is an enormous task all by itself. Instead, we will summarize some of the works of the past ECK Masters, and their lives throughout history.

Among the early ECK Masters was Ramaj who came out of the dark forest of what is now Germany, and made his way East. He entered first into Persia and established the Magi Order, centuries before the birth of Zoroaster, the great Persian sage. Then he went into India and there founded the Indian religion, which is an offshoot of ECK.

Gopal Das, great ECK Master and guardian of the Temple of Golden Wisdom on the astral plane, lived in Egypt in 3000 B.C., when the Pyramids were being built by the Pharaohs at Sakkara. He founded the mystery cults of Osiris and Isis.

When he departed from this world his place was taken by Moraji Desal. This was during that period in history when Hammurabi ruled the Semitic kingdom of Babylon, and the land of Canaan was part of his empire. This was about 2067-2025 B.C., at the time of Abraham. Moraji Desal was a wanderer who traveled most of the kingdom by foot preaching ECKANKAR to all who would listen. Although he helped write the great Hammurabic Code of

Laws he was hunted much of the time by the priestcraft, who believed he was preaching a pagan religion.

His spiritual mantle was turned over to Shiv Sena, a Hindu, who was a prominent leader of the ECK faith. He inspired Moses to lead the Israelites out of Egypt. He was also responsible for such marvelous miracles as the opening of the Red Sea and it was he who advised Moses to go to the mountain where the Ten Commandments were revealed and given to the people.

He eventually retired into the spiritual worlds to work under the Deity Sat Nam, on the fifth plane.

His place was taken by Yaubl Sacabi, whose work was among the Mycenaeans who invaded Greece during the period between 2000-1700 B. C. By spreading ECK he became the leading figure among the Greek mystery cults during the early history of the coun'ry. Out of this grew the exceedingly fine culture which has since shaped Western civilization. Given the choice to either work in the spiritual world or stay in this physical region, he chose the latter and became the guardian of the part of the Shariyat-Ki-Sugmad taught at the spiritual city of Agam Des in the Himalayan mountains. This is also the home of the Eshwar-Khanewale, the God-Eaters, for they partake of the cosmic spirit as we do material foods.

He has immortalized his body and is still living in it. His age is beyond the concepts of human imagination.

When he left this sphere of influence the title of Mahanta was turned over to Hari Tita, who was one of the greats during the Trojan period of Greek history. He ascended into heaven and does his work in the Alakh Lok region.

Following Hari Tita came Lamotta, who accepted the spiritual mantle in the year 1000 B.C. and tried to spread ECK throughout the world. He was hunted down and slain by bands of Assyrians during the time of David the King, and when he passed on, his duties were established to assist Rami Nuri on Venus to teach the Shariyat-Ki-Sugmad to those who come there to learn.

189

Sardar Lhunpo served as the living ECK Master in Rome during the early years of the Republic. He went into the causal world to work in ECK.

Vajra Manjushri was the ECK Master in approximately 700 B. C., in Persia. He tried to teach ECKANKAR openly to the Persians but they were too enmeshed in Mithraism. Through the instigation of a priest of Mithra he was arrested by King Hakhamanish I, and executed. He is now teaching in the causal world.

Padma Gaya was at Nineveh when it was destroyed by the Babylonians in 612 B. C., and later watched the building of the Hanging Gardens by Nebuchadnezzar. He was also present when Solomon's Temple was destroyed.

During the time of Buddha, in India, the Master Fubbi Quantz served. At the completion of his mission he immortalized his body and became Abbot of the Katsupari Monastery where another section of the famed Shariyat-Ki-Sugmad is located.

The ECK Master Chu-Ko Yen was an associate of Confucius in China. He guided the Chinese Master by giving him spiritual advice in his work to reach the world and form a greater society. He passed on and became a spiritual guide on the Alakh Lok.

When Darius the Great and his army of Persians fought at Marathon in 490 B. C., and began to march on Athens, the living ECK Master sat on a street corner in the Greek capitol and prophesied the defeat of Darius. This was Habu Medinet, one of the greatest of all ECK Masters. He is now serving the SUGMAD on the mental plane in the Temple of Golden Wisdom in the city of Mer Kailash, under Towart Managi.

His successor was Jagat Ho, a high spiritual traveler who lived and died in China during the years 490-438 B.C. He went to the etheric plane where he is a co-worker in the Temple of Golden Wisdom under Lai Tsi.

He passed his spiritual title to Philias the Greek, who was the sculptor of the Parthenon in Athens. He supervised the Doric design of the most famous building in the ancient world, the "Temple of the Goddess Athena." He tried to put into this temple his ideal of the ECK, and one who is fortunate enough to see and study the Parthenon will find the ancient mysteries of ECK.

Athena was one of the earliest followers of ECKAN-KAR. She is considered a legend belonging to Greek mythology, but she was, nevertheless, a flesh and blood woman who had much of the power of ECK in her grasp, although she was not an ECK Master.

Following Philias came the living ECK Master Vaita Danu, who lived during the time of Alexander the Great. A Hindu, Vaita Danu was present during Alexander's march into India. He lived for more than one hundred and fifty years because of his great knowledge of the Ayur Vedha, a system for renewing body health.

When Alexander entered into India and conquered the lands east of the Indus River, he settled his armies into camp to rest. It was then that Vaita Danu appeared before him, with a sack of water. "Drink this, Alexander," he said, "and all life will be yours."

The ECK was testing Alexander, for if he were to drink of the water offered him, this famed conqueror would be released from his insatiable desire for conquest. His spiritual eye would have been opened, giving him immortality of Soul. Instead, he hesitated, thinking the offer was a deception of some nature. Within that moment of hesitation, one of his officers sliced the water bag with his sword, thinking it contained poison.

As the water spilled upon the ground Vaita Danu said, "You have been tested and found wanting, Sire. You shall die early in life, unhappy that no worlds are yours for conquering. You shall become a wanderer through life, in birth after birth, until you find One who will take you to the SUGMAD."

He disappeared into thin air just as the officer poised to strike him with the sword.

Ju Chiao followed him as the living ECK Master. He was a young fisherman who took up the call during the Punic Wars between Rome and Carthage. Restless for an understanding of life, he became a warrior under Hannibal but learned that his search for life lay beyond this. He was initiated by Vaita Danu who gave him the spiritual mantle on his departure from this world. But Hannibal did not like the teachings of Ju Chiao and had him killed.

During the time of Julius Caesar the living ECK Master was Ori Diogo, who lived quietly in Rome. He foretold the death of Caesar by the Ides of March. Few knew him, but he helped shape much of the world in those days for spiritual advancement.

He chose his work on the astral plane where he has charge of healing for those who come across after death from some accident, disease, or other affliction.

Zadok followed Ori Diogo. He was living, at the time of his ECK Mastership, in the country of Judea, north of Jerusalem. His work was with a small group of followers who had broken with the Essenes, a mystic order of the times. They grew in large numbers as a secret, mystical organization which exists to this day in the Middle East. They accept the living ECK Master as the Mahanta, for through a secret inner communication channel they always keep in touch with the Master.

Zadok saw the man named Jesus, talked with Him on several occasions, and knew His purpose in this world. He also knew that their missions did not cross. Neither of them had any physical contact with each other after Jesus left the ECK group, with whom he studied for some time under the great Zadok. The ECK Master gave Jesus the basic fundamentals of ECKANKAR, who used them in His own teachings. Out of His knowledge of ECK came what we know today as Christianity.

During the reign of Constantine the Great the living ECK Master was Babla Mohenjo, who was one of Its greatest teachers. He had a small school for ECK chelas near Constantinople. He was at the Council of Nicaea called by Constantine in Bithynia, Asia Minor, during 325 A.D., to get Christians to settle their quarrels and support the empire.

He was not at all in favor of what went on at the Council, but he never interfered.

Joyti Basji was living ECK Master during the extension of the Mayan empire from the Yucatan and Guatemala into the heart of Mexico. He was responsible for re-establishing the ECK mysteries which had died out somewhat after another ECK Master, Quetzalcoatl, had formed the religion of the empire centuries before. He had left Atlantis just prior to the destruction of that unhappy continent, and had gone to Mexico to establish the mysteries of ECK. This was around the year 1055, B.C.

Many others appeared between this time and during the reign of Charlemagne the Great. Then there appeared the marvelous living ECK Master Ketu Jaraul who became the secret advisor of Charlemagne for all matters. He taught the Emperor the secrets of ECK and helped him in spiritual problems.

Priscus followed Ketu Jaraul. He is not to be confused with Priscus Hevidius, the ECK Master who was a Roman Senator during the time of Emperor Vespasian, in 69 A.D. "Priscus" is the only name that this Master adopted. He was in England at the time of its conquest by William of Normandy, and at the gathering in France in 1096 where Peter the Hermit preached support for the First Crusade. He accompanied this First Crusade and died in the Holy Lands.

Milarepa was the wonderful ECK Master living in Tibet in the twelfth century whose life reads like a storybook. He began life as a black magician but later became the spectacular saint of Tibet. His secret life was concerned with ECK-ANKAR.

Ahmad Qavani, the living ECK Master during the time of King John of England, was present at the signing of the Magna Charta.

Rebazar Tarzs was born in the year of 1461, in the mountain village of Sarana in northern Tibet. He developed into mastership under the spiritual guidance of Yaubl Sacabi. It was he who was responsible for Christopher Columbus' inner guidance. He stayed on earth for seventy-five years teaching

ECK, then he retired in the same body to the mountainous vastness of the Himalayas. He has spiritually developed several ECK Masters, and is responsible for passing the Rod of ECK power from one Master to his successor. He also developed spiritually Peddar Zaskq.

During the early conquest of Mexico and Southwest America, the living ECK Master was Vardrup, who lived in Germany and came to the Americas to give spiritual aid. He raised several Indian chiefs to a high place in the spiritual worlds, as well as many Europeans and Asiatics.

The next ECK Master of importance to this study is Tissot Leins, who lived during the sixteenth century in France, when the Protestants were being persecuted. He was responsible for the migration of the Huguenots and those of other faiths to America.

During the seventeenth century Ismet Houdoni was the ECK Master, who served while the settlements of Jamestown and Plymouth were being nurtured in America. He served James I of England as an advisor, and led him into making an English version of the Bible. He lived to an age of one hundred thirty-five, then entered into the causal plane to work for the cause of ECK.

Next is Hipolito Fayolle, who served during the eighteenth century. He came into this world on a small farm near Dresden, Germany, in the usual manner of the ECK Masters —very mysteriously. Few know how they are given birth, but always some family adopts them during their infancy and while raising them, one member of the family who is adept at Soul Travel teaches them at an early age. Most ECK Masters are born either in the high mountains or on some body of water. Hipolito Fayolle lived to the age of ninety-seven and lifted many ECK chelas into the higher worlds. Most of his outer works corncerned European and American political figures. He went into the inner worlds to work on the Alakh Lok plane.

The next living ECK Master pertinent to our study is the very famous Janos Moneta, an entity who influenced the early eighteenth century by breaking up all the old established forms of religion, music and art. He had deep spiritual influence upon the early part of the century. He lived in Sweden near Stockholm, and was a friend of Swedenborg, who studied ECKANKAR. Much of Swedenborg's life and writings show the influence of Janos Moneta. When the Master passed on he went into the mental plane to work.

During the middle and later part of the nineteenth century Yu Rantga, a Chinese master, lived in the Gobi Desert and was the living ECK Master of his times. During the civil war that caused so much bloodshed he brought back to the Chinese many of their old religious customs, and gave the masses spiritual succor. He left this world after seventy-two years of service and went to the astral plane to work.

The next Master was Sudar Singh of Allahabad who spread ECK to Europe and other places on the globe. He lived into his nineties before passing away.

Following him is Peddar Zaskq, who was born on a packetboat in the midst of the Mississippi River, a few minutes after a great earthquake shook the mid-South and formed a great lake in this region. He became the Mahanta, the living ECK Master after studying under Rebazar Tarzs.

This is, briefly, the history of the living ECK Masters who have lived in this world. I have not included those who served between the years and centuries left blank in this summary.

Too many persons try to substitute orthodox teachings for ECKANKAR. Too many go to cults, thinking they have found the way for themselves. But each of those who leave the path of ECK, or refuse to accept the living ECK Master, will come to grief upon the rocks as surely as a captain wrecks his ship on the reef by not listening to the pilot.

Again and again I have pointed out that there is no other path than ECK. It is the original source from which all things spring, and anyone who tries another path is trying to start on a lower rung. It seems so foolish for anyone to use his human judgment in trying to select a spiritual path for himself, when it is laid out for him to move onto the original and only path to God.

Within the Shariyat-Ki-Sugmad is found the quotation, "He who leaves the path of ECK, or refuses to follow it, shall dwell in the astral hells until the Master takes mercy upon him and brings him upon the path again. But he shall first ask the Master to be compassionate; to give him spiritual aid and take him into the light of God again."

No one escapes the suffering that he brings upon himself. If he tries to mix the ECK teachings with any system, the same results become apparent. He must realize that the discipline of ECK is for his own spiritual good and he should never flinch. Otherwise troubles will begin that have no ending until the day comes when he turns again to the living ECK Master and asks to be taken back.

The field of mystical or religious experiences has always been left to the saints, mystics and masters. But the ECK has resolved it so that the individual who takes up this particular but only path to God can also have the same experience. The living ECK Master rids the chela of whatever has aberrated him, by fasting for the chela or getting him out of his abortive state of consciousness.

The Order of the Vairagi is the only pure line of spiritual Masters in the world. Although I did not go into any of the very ancient periods of Lemuria or Atlantis, nevertheless, the living ECK Masters were prominent. Some persons have tried to identify the Masters with other ancient cults but they must always remember that ECK is the pure line, the original source out of which all life, religions and philosophies have sprung. Once they accept this, then all things fall into line. Every religion, every cult, and every philosophy is only an echo or mirror of ECKANKAR.

Ramaji was one of the first initiates in the ancient Order of the Vairagi. Before him was Dayaka, who was a great ECK Master in Lemuria. Then there was Kassapa, the living ECK Master who preceded the antediluvian disaster of Atlantis. The line can be traced all the way back to Gakko who came out of the heart of God into this world about six million years ago. The whole line of ECK Masters has descended from him in an unbroken lineage.

Some have been married men, others single. But they have all served the ECK faithfully, giving their full lives to It. Some have lived out lives of longevity like Yaubl Sacabi, Fubbi Quantz and Rebazar Tarzs, or the ancient ECK Master Asoki, who was born during the time of the large empire of Uighur in Central Asia. This was part of the vast empire we know as Mu, or Lemuria. Asoki is still living in the same body he inhabited in those ancient days, some sixty thousand years before the advent of the Christian calendar. He lives near the city of Retz, the capitol of Venus. His duties in this universe are to help spread the message of ECK throughout the physical world and the planets.

Each living ECK Master has become the Mahanta, which is God made flesh on Earth. Therefore, we look to the Mahanta for he is the representative of the Sugmad in our midst today. He has what is known as a quinbody, which goes beyond the trinity. All religions speak of the trinity or the tribodies of their spiritual leaders, but the Mahanta is beyond any of this for he uses the quinbodies as his vehicles. They are: the physical, the astral, the causal, the mental, and the Soul body. He sometimes operates in quinbodies such as the physical, psychic, Soul and reality Itself.

ECK only interests us in the fifth world. This is what we are trying to establish here and now. It means that everybody chooses that part of Truth he interprets to be in his best interest. If he cannot get interested in the fifth world, as presented him by ECK, he loses faith and disintegrates in personality and self.

There are three outstanding factors in ECKANKAR. They are: the spiritual exercises of ECK, the constant presence of the Mahanta, and the chela doing all activities in the name of the Master.

These are most important in the life of the chela. It means he must first recognize the Mahanta's presence in every moment of his life. Second, the chela must practice his spiritual exercises faithfully, and third, he must do everything

197

with a love for the Master. This latter point is certainly the most important for the chela. He must think that everything he does consciously and subconsciously is for the Master and in the Master's name. Unless he does this he will lose some of his spiritual unfoldment. He will come to a standstill and wonder what is wrong within himself.

He must realize the five basic points of ECK. They are as follows:

1. ECK is the ancient, original essence which sustains life in all universes.

2. ECK is the ancient teaching that is the source from which all religions and philosophies spring.

3. The living ECK Master is the only manifestation of the SUGMAD on Earth, and the basis of his teachings lie in the inner Master.

4. The living ECK Master's only mission is to gather up Souls who are ready, and start them on the path to God again.

5. The living ECK Master is the perfect instrument of the SUGMAD on this plane, often he is the Mahanta. His duty is to make every Soul who comes to him realize he has only one mission in life, and that is to return to God and likewise become an instrument of God.

These are the basic principles of ECK. One should have them well grounded within himself and know each one of them by heart. For once one realizes what they mean and actually understands them, he then will begin to know the true meaning of Soul Travel; the true meaning of the ECK.

ECK has no symbol but It, of Itself. All religions and philosophies have some sort of symbol or talisman which bespeaks of the Godhead. But since the ECK is the Godhead of Itself, there is no symbol but the ECK. It is very hard to say just what is a symbol for Truth.

The ancient people used certain symbols in their ceremonies like the Masons do in their lodge meetings. But ECK cannot have any symbol for It is what It is! If God IS, then ECK is what It is. It cannot be anything else but this.

198

The origin of religion lies in the factor of symbolism. There was a primitive ECK teaching before the Aryan, Semitic, or Tauranian religions existed. It was broken up, though, because of the cataclysmic upheavals that caused separate races, languages, worship and national sentiment.

This goes back into the misty dawn of time before history was ever recorded. During those early days the universal God was a part of man's search and It still is, even though he does not know exactly what he has been seeking due to lack of inner experience.

The history of the human race is a collective story of man's desperate attempt to find a solution to this search. He has failed because few, if any, cultures have laid down a yardstick by which to measure their successes and failures at God-Realization. All through mythology this universal God has received a name. The Greeks called It Zeus; the Latin name was Jove; It was Wotan in German; and in Sanskrit It was known as Dyaus.

The Universal name for this highest Deity has always been the "Heavenly Father." All gave It a masculine gender. This, of course, has never been true for the SUGMAD, which is ITS true name, is neuter in nature. It is neither masculine nor feminine. Someone asked at one time if the female can go beyond the Soul plane. No, the feminine self cannot do this, but neither can the masculine. Only the neuter self can. Once Soul reaches the fifth plane, then it becomes the neuter self and enters into the greater realms of God. But never as masculine or feminine. This should resolve many of the questions that arose in the minds of readers who have studied The Tiger's Fang.

The five problems of the human state of consciousness are loneliness, death, despair, dread and anxiety. They are the attributes of the Kal power and if one does not practice the spiritual exercises of ECK he will most likely become enmeshed in these aspects. Then instead of becoming an instrument of God, he becomes the channel for Kal. The conflict spoken of in the previous chapter takes over, splitting one's outer personality so that he may even become a victim of society and placed in a mental institution. This is certainly true in various professions today.

Many persons who wish to take up the study of spiritual works should really remain with some orthodox religion. A world-wide religion such as Catholicism or Buddhism is a stabilizing force for many people, and they should not venture any further than this. Otherwise, they may become very disturbed as they are opened to psychic forces, and they are likely to be pushed over the borderline between normalcy and neurosis. It is regrettable that the public must be exposed to misbehaviour by such people. Entertainers and movie stars frequently have the problem of psychic disturbance, as well as rock groups, actors, musicians, protestors and certain others in the public eye.

We have now what is known as a paranoid society. The mistake we have made is that the physical universe has established an educational standard that only sharpens the intellect and offers little spiritual development for students. Many believe that the intellect is the criteria for spiritual unfoldment; that it makes them superior to the laws of society. They feel they are outside of social laws and can upset and disturb, control and manipulate the social forces of life. This is only an illusion of the Kal power. Since Kal Niranjan is the King of the negative world, he has the ultimate power over the senses and intellectual faculties. It is strange that these highly educated people do not see this.

It is for this reason that many ECK Masters are not educated according to the social standards of their times. Academic, institutional education is the way of the negative. But we can neither brush it aside nor ignore it, because one has to live in this world. As long as society demands that the individual have a standard of education in order to fit into its ways, then all must have one to make his own way in the negative worlds. But for those who are spiritually developed to a high degree, academic education is not necessary. These persons find a way to live in our social order yet not be a part of it. They still live within the social laws yet they have spiritual freedom.

We must realize that the parapsychologists have been making a major error in their experimentations with the psychic sciences. They have been trying to measure the effects of psychic power with the laws of the material universe. Since the psychic power and its aspects are beyond the physical senses, it follows that no law of this world is capable of measuring its effects. And this is where the advocates of academic educational standards make their mistake. No society for physical research, nor any university department on parapsychology, is able to take a correct measurement or make an authentic test in either the psychic or the spiritual sciences.

They might think that what they are doing is right, but it never measures up in the long run. They count the failures, but never the successes, of anyone who is in either field. It is a mistake for any spiritually developed individual to subject himself to any tests of this nature.

This, however, does not resolve the usual problems of mankind which I spoke of previously. They are again: loneliness, death, despair, dread, and anxiety.

In fact, neither parapsychology nor any of the other sciences have ever yet found an answer for any of these age old problems. These problems can be overcome, though, in ECK. Once man has learned to travel into the other worlds, he finds his attention is no longer placed on the negative aspects of life.

In the inner worlds one finds companionship, life, hope, love, peace and self-reliance. No spiritual path can promise this for they have no techniques, no understanding of how to find the answer to overcome the negative. Since human consciousness is a negative state of being, man can never use it to find what he is seeking until he seeks instead spiritual consciousness.

When one reaches the spiritual state of consciousness via ECK, he learns many things he could not have understood in his human state. He now knows that the ECK Master does not, nor did he ever, have a Soul mate, as many people believe. Since the ECK Master is the ECK, the living Word, he could not have a Soul mate, ever. Nor has he ever been linked with anyone in the past, as either a human mate, a relative, or family member. His only connection with anyone is as the Mahanta, the living ECK Master.

The same force, the ECK, polarizes Itself time and again in the human body, which is the living ECK Master of any and every period in history. The human self of the living ECK Master is only superfluous and should be regarded as such. What is important to every individual who is an ECK chela is the Mahanta, the inner Master.

It makes little difference whether the person who is interested in ECK has read only one book, has just become an initiate, or has passed through all the initiations, the ECK Master is with him constantly. When the student becomes an aspirant in the Satsang discourses, he can expect the ECK Master to become as much a part of him and guide him as much inwardly as the highest chela in the ECK movement. It makes little difference to the Master who the devotee might be; that individual gets the full protection of the Master's power, and the Master's complete love.

One of the ways to understand the ECK Master's love is called the Tawaga, the Master's gaze. It is important to note this, for the subtle knowledge of his loving look at an individual can heal, give spiritual aid and upliftment, or remove karmic burdens. Once the chela learns the importance of the Master's gaze or the slightest touch of the Master's hand, it becomes a unique knowledge that no others possess. He knows the inner value of being near the Master in heart, mind and Soul. He knows and understands the true meaning of being opened to the Mahanta, the inner Master, who can perform miracles.

The Mahanta is the only being who can perform any miracles. All others are only psychic phenomena. It is he who gives the initiation to the chela and reveals the sacred mysteries of ECK through inner communication. When he announces that the chela is ready for the initiation, his word is final and there is never to be any hesitation on the part of the chela

Once the chela is initiated into ECK, he becomes a part of the inner house. He lives beyond his physical senses in the House of God whether he knows this consciously or not. If the chela should, by any desire, wish to withdraw from his spiritual home, it is entirely his own decision and the Master never interferes. But he forgets that if he does this, he re-enters the world and must take his load of karma which the Master accepted upon initiation.

If he leaves the House of ECK his suffering begins, for he has descended the ladder instead of climbing, as he should. He is like the swimmer who gets half way across the river and then turns back, fearful of losing strength to finish the task. He forgets that the swim back is also as long and arduous as crossing the river in the first place.

If one goes ahead on the path of ECK and follows the spiritual guidance of the Master, he will eventually reach the ultimate awareness of God.

The path lies through the Mahanta, the living ECK Master, via the ECK, the audible life current. The Mahanta will guide the chela over the rocky path into the heart of the SUGMAD.

He will become the co-worker of God.

He will dwell in eternity in peace and happiness.

INDEX

209

211

O

Objective
  Sight, 13
  View, 79, 85
  World, 24, 33, 41
Obstacles, 49, 124
Ocean of Love & Mercy, 9,
  11, 107, 148, 183
Occult Practices, 36, 90,
  102, 112
Old, New Testament, 27,
  166, 169
Omnipotence, Omnipresence,
  Omniscience, 52, 58
Opposite Poles, 60, 88
Oracle of Tirmer (Tibet),
  130, 152
Oracles, 8
Oral Instructions, 120, 123
Original Cause, 54, 70, 86
Orpheus, 6

P

Pain, 60, 63, 161, 168
Paradise, 37, 47
Par Brahm (Ruler, Etheric)
  105
Param-Sant, 19
Passions, 60, 71
Passivity, 94, 115
Past Lives, 71, 90, 104, 108,
  116, 140, 142, 152
Pasteur, 161
Pavlov, 143
Peace of Mind, 105, 110, 114,
  146, 147

Perceptiveness, 133
Perfection, 22, 137, 157
Persia, 10, 146, 158, 167
Personality, 79, 140, 141,
  147
Petition, Four Levels of, 91,
  158
Philosophical Concepts, 49,
  104, 115, 168
Phoenicians, 8
Physical
  Embodiment, 34, 54, 80,
    85, 86, 109, 112, 160,
    163, 171
  Environment, 89, 90
  Fatigue, 49
  Force, 70
  Illness, 161
  Image, 139
  Karma, 84, 86
  Life, 16, 34, 37, 54, 107
  Losses, 62
  Plane, 35, 53, 67, 68, 85,
    144
  Reaction, 125
  Senses, 33, 59, 71, 72, 78,
    109, 125, 132, 134
  Torture, 143
Pilgrim's Progress, 49
Pinda (Physical Universe), 39
  93, 104
Pineal Gland, 93
Planes, Names & Sounds of,
  101-117
Planetary Spirit, 90
Planets
  Earth, 39, 87, 110, 159
  Mars, 64

213

216

217

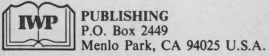

BOOK ORDER COUPON

Mail to:

 PUBLISHING
P.O. Box 2449
Menlo Park, CA 94025 U.S.A.

☐ Please send me a complete IWP catalog.

I enclose $_____ for the book(s) checked below.

Foreign countries: Please remit Int'l M.O. or
check payable in U.S. funds to IWP PUBLISHING.

0104	_____	**In My Soul I Am Free** $2.95	$_____
0106	_____	**The Tiger's Fang** $2.50 papbk	_____
010699	_____	**The Tiger's Fang** $8.95 hb	_____
0110	_____	**Your Right to Know** $1.95 papbk	_____
011099	_____	**Your Right to Know** $8.95 hb	_____
011299	_____	**From Heaven to the Prairie** $14.95	_____
0126	_____	**The Flute of God** $2.95	_____
0128	_____	**The Spiritual Notebook** $2.95	_____
0132	_____	**Stranger by the River** $5.95	_____
0154	_____	**Letters to Gail, Vol. I** $5.95 papbk	_____
0155	_____	**Letters to Gail, Vol. II** $9.95 hb	_____
0188	_____	**The Wind of Change** $3.95 papbk	_____
018899	_____	**The Wind of Change** $6.95 hb	_____

Total $_____

6% sales tax (California only) $_____

Add 10% for shipping $_____
75¢ minimum

TOTAL ENCLOSED $_____

Name _____
(please print)

Street _____

City _____ State_____

Country _____ Postal Code_____

(detach here)

999903

— detach here —